Out of Apath

Out of Apathy

Voices of the New Left
Thirty Years On

◆

*Papers based on a Conference
organized by the*
OXFORD UNIVERSITY
SOCIALIST DISCUSSION GROUP

Edited by

Robin Archer
Diemut Bubeck
Hanjo Glock
Lesley Jacobs
Seth Moglen
Adam Steinhouse
Daniel Weinstock

VERSO
London · New York

First published by Verso 1989

Verso
UK: 6 Meard Street, London W1V 3HR
USA: 29 West 35th Street, New York, NY 10001-2291

Verso is the imprint of New Left Books

British Library Cataloguing in Publication Data

Out of apathy: voices of the New Left 30 years on: papers based on a conference
organised by the Oxford University Socialist Discussion Group.
1. Western World. New Left movement. Political ideologies
I. Archer, Robin II. University of Oxford,
Socialist Discussion Group
320.5′3′091821

ISBN 0-86091-232-9
ISBN 0-86091-945-5 Pbk

US Library of Congress Cataloguing in Publication Data

Out of apathy: voices of the new Left thirty years on: papers based
on the conference organized by the Oxford University Socialist
Discussion Group/edited by Robin Archer . . . [et al.].
        p.   cm.
    Includes index.
    ISBN 0-86091-232-9—ISBN 0-86091-945-5 (pbk.)
        1. New Left—Great Britain—Congresses.   2. Socialism—Great
Britain—Congresses.   3. Socialists—Great Britain—Congresses.
I. Archer, Robin.   II. Oxford University Socialist Discussion Group.
HX244.098   1989
335′.00941—dc20

Typeset by Leaper & Gard Limited, Bristol, England

Printed and bound in Great Britain by
Marston Book Services Ltd, Oxfordshire

Contents

Preface

It is not often that the builders of a political movement reassemble after several decades to discuss their common efforts, to evaluate successes and failures, to identify points of continuing growth and points of ending. The 'Out of Apathy' conference which was held in Oxford on 14 November 1987 provided such a moment of self-evaluation for the early British New Left. The conference brought together for the first time in thirty years the intellectuals, artists and activists who set in motion the first phase of the movement in the late 1950s.

The event was not intended as an exercise in nostalgia, nor merely as a historical retrospective. Neither was it a unified meeting with a common aim: no manifestoes were delivered, no platform was launched or reaffirmed. It was, rather, a moment of critical reflection by the founders of a movement which has exerted a sustained influence on left politics and culture in Britain during the last three decades. Participants at the conference were asked to reflect on the contemporary significance of the early New Left's ideas and experiences, and to draw some lessons from the movement's development which could be applied to the situation that we face on the left today. This book is a record of that moment of self-evaluation.

The form of this record has had to be flexible enough to accommodate its varied and often informal material: the book is neither a transcript of the conference proceedings nor a planned collection of formal essays. Most of the chapters mirror the topical sessions of the 'Out of Apathy' conference, with most of the original presentations having been written up as papers. Chapters 3, 8 and 9 provide transcribed material in lightly edited form.

The editors would like to acknowledge at the outset that neither the original 'Out of Apathy' conference, nor this book which emerges from it, can make any claim of completeness in its representation of the early New Left. While many of the influential writers and activists from this first phase attended the conference and have made contributions here, some others were inevitably absent. Despite our attempts to keep representation from the two original New Left journals equal, voices from *Universities and Left Review* proved more numerous than those from *The New Reasoner*. Because the two journals differed substantially in their political emphases, constituency and tone, this imbalance is unfortunate.

The position and experience of women in the early New Left raised particular problems of representation. Because the conference organization emphasized the importance of the journals, in which relatively few women published, and of theoretical debates in particular, in which even fewer women participated, the event regrettably reproduced the stark gender imbalance present in early New Left publications. An explosive session at the conference explicitly raised the question of the relative silence and invisibility of women in the early years of the movement, and we have added a chapter (6) in which women speak directly to this issue.

Despite the inevitable gaps in this record, we hope that the book draws some useful lines of connection, and establishes some points of contact, between the politics of the first New Left and the politics of the present. At a time of rethinking on the left, it is perhaps particularly appropriate for the first New Left, after thirty years, to name weaknesses and to reaffirm strengths.

Acknowledgements

This book is only the most visible outcome of three years of ongoing discussions in the Oxford University Socialist Discussion Group. For this reason we want to acknowledge the contributions of all members of the group, past and present. We owe a particular debt to Robin Archer, who initiated the group and sustained it in its early years. We would also like to thank the participants in the early New Left who advised us throughout the project and gave us encouragement. Not least, we want to extend our thanks to the organizers, speakers and other participants, who made the conference a successful and exciting event. Finally, we would like to express our gratitude to Verso, the imprint of New Left Books, for their patience and for publishing this book from a sense of political and historical commitment.

Special mention should be made of Seth Moglen, who, as coordinating editor, rescued the book project from the spreading apathy of the editorial group, and spent much more time and energy than any of us to make sure the book materialized.

Introduction

How will the historian describe our times? . . . The Age of Apathy?
Or the age in which the rebellion of Socialist Humanism began?

Edward Thompson, *Out of Apathy* (1960)

Those of us who organized the 'Out of Apathy' conference and who
have edited this book are outsiders to the New Left. It seems
appropriate, therefore, to offer some explanation for why we – an
international group of graduate students from a new political generation
– should have thought it important today to bring together the founders of
the British New Left.

This project has been part of the ongoing work of the Oxford
University Socialist Discussion Group. The group was formed by graduate students in response to the limitations and rigidities of Oxford,
where the great bulk of social and political thought takes place within a
liberal framework. In the last few years, the Socialist Discussion Group
has provided an alternative forum within the university for the open
exploration of socialist ideas. The group has no affiliation with any
political party. Our work is informed by the conviction that continued
adherence to the dogmas and orthodoxies of the past only inhibits an
urgently needed renewal of socialist thought.

Our group was drawn to the early New Left for a variety of reasons.
First, we perceive a significant parallel between the situation confronting
the left throughout the West today and that faced by the founders of the
early New Left in the late 1950s. The parallel is perhaps most sharply
illustrated in the British context. The 'Out of Apathy' conference took
place within months of the Labour Party's third consecutive general
election defeat. Not since 1959 has the left in Britain had to come to
terms with such demoralizing circumstances. Just as then, the very

meaning of socialism has been thrown into doubt; just as then, a loud chorus predicts its demise. Those of us who remain committed to the values which have motivated socialist movements face the pressing challenge of reconstructing a coherent political programme, and of shaping a new left politics which genuinely addresses modern needs. Our group wanted to see what could be learned from a previous generation of committed activists and intellectuals who found themselves in a similar situation thirty years ago and created, from the midst of confusion, a sense of renewal on the left. The social energy and the enthusiasm which the early New Left inspired seems to have stemmed from the movement's radical questioning of received orthodoxies and from its reaffirmation of socialism's humanist traditions.

Second, some of the central ideas and concerns of the New Left have become so widespread that they form an important part of the political culture in which we ourselves are steeped. The first British New Left marked an important early stage in the larger formation of post-war New Left politics (a formation itself influenced in the late 1950s by the even earlier stirrings of the *nouvelle gauche* in France and by such maverick leftists as C. Wright Mills in the USA). The values and emphases of the early British New Left not only exercised great influence on the movement's later incarnation in Britain, but also fertilized the radical politics of the 1960s in North America and in Europe. The social movements of the 1970s and 1980s, which have decisively shaped the political consciousness of our generation, extended this New Left tradition further and in some new directions.

We stand, therefore, rather a long way down a road which the founders of the early New Left began to travel. Some of the ideas which they formulated have become political assumptions in our generation. While there are features of early New Left thought which, with historical hindsight, we would criticize or disregard, there are also important elements of the New Left heritage which we share: a commitment to radical democracy; a sense that open theoretical debate can and should play a role in the development of practical politics; a suspicion of social democratic parties and a sympathetic interest in emerging social movements. To rethink socialism today, one must employ terms which the New Left has made common currency and assess ideas and political realities which the early New Left helped to bring into being.

Third, and at a rather different level, the early New Left represents for some of us a model of politically engaged intellectual questioning. The movement initiated an open discourse about Marxism and socialist politics free from the power struggles of political parties, but none the less attempting to make serious contributions to both political thought and political action. The New Left refused to restrict itself either to the distant language of academia or to the internal arguments of established parties, but sought rather to inspire a broad and genuine debate about political values and priorities. Because they believed that ideas shape political realities, members of the early New Left wrote and spoke about ideas as if they mattered. Today, when most political discourse seems again restricted either to the banalities of party politics or to the scholasticism of an increasingly alienated academia, the intellectual vitality of the early New Left provides a refreshing model of politically meaningful intellectual work.

Finally, we believe that some basic ideas and emphases of the early New Left deserve reaffirmation today. This is not to say that we think the movement's banners should be dragged out and waved again. Inevitably, many of its practical policy initiatives are now dated, and some of the political and ideological campaigns which it fought so strenuously in the winter of the Cold War have lost relevance in an altered political situation. Nevertheless, we do feel great respect for the basic moral and political commitments which gave content to the movement.

Raphael Samuel observed at the 'Out of Apathy' conference that 'the New Left defined not so much a politics but a stance; it was concerned not so much to establish a platform but to open up a space.' As Stuart Hall explains in his introductory chapter, this open space was seen in the early years of the movement as a 'third space' between the two existing Cold War socialist alternatives – Stalinism and social democracy. The urgent need for such a space arose in part from the dramatic historical events of 1956. On the one hand, the revelations of Khrushchev's 'secret speech' at the CPSU's Twentieth Party Congress and the Soviet Union's invasion of Hungary drove thousands of independently minded socialists out of the British Communist Party. On the other hand, the joint Anglo-French attack on Suez, and the British Labour Party's support for it, revealed to many that the post-war social democratic consensus was implicated in promoting a new stage of imperialism. The impoverishment of social democracy was further demonstrated domestically by the compromised position offered by such leading figures as Gaitskell and Crosland, who seemed to suggest that the goals of socialism had been largely achieved by welfare-state capitalism.

Out of this political crisis, the New Left emerged with a strong sense of the moral and political failure of post-war socialism. In different ways, both Stalinism and social democracy had betrayed the humanist impulse which the founders of the New Left regarded as the essence of the socialist tradition. Perhaps most fundamentally, the New Left movement was an attempt to reaffirm the humanist values which it saw as lying at the heart of the socialist ideal, and to re-establish a politics in the radical space which those values defined.

The New Left project was characterized by a distinctive concern with human liberation and a moral commitment to human agency. The movement condemned Stalinism and social democracy because both, in different ways, failed to promote people's capacity to control their own lives. The New Left sought to return to the centre of left politics the image of human beings as individuals both worthy and capable of shaping their own destiny.

This insistence on human agency found expression through a variety of closely linked intellectual and political projects. In their most philosophical mode, New Left writers attempted to articulate a conception of socialist humanism. At another level, the movement broke with the reductionist 'base–superstructure' model of orthodox Marxism, and initiated a sophisticated analysis of culture as the sphere in which men and women actively create their identities and define their forms of social organization. This analysis led to a radical expansion of the New Left's conception of politics and the addition of 'cultural' issues to the political agenda. Their liberationist ethic also informed practical policy initiatives and political campaigns, from workers' self-management to 'positive neutralism', which emphasized the importance of democratic self-determination and the liberation of individual creative energies.

The ideal of socialist humanism provided the theoretical cornerstone of the early New Left. As advocated by a number of contributors to *Universities and Left Review (ULR)* and *The New Reasoner* (and in a particularly sustained way by Edward Thompson), socialist humanism affirmed human agency against what was identified as the determinist politics of Stalinism and social democracy. The critique of Stalinist orthodoxy condemned the faith in a 'scientific socialism' in the name of which so many thousands had died, and under the pretext of which authoritarianism had eclipsed humanism. The critique of social democracy condemned a politics in which political decisions were taken through bureaucratic rather than democratic process; in which technocratic 'expediency' and instrumental 'necessities' replaced free moral choices.

As a result of its virtually universal acceptance, this critique of Stalinist orthodoxy has lost much of its urgency in the 1980s. However, the New Left's critique of social democracy, which focused on the widespread apathy produced by an ideology of political expediency, speaks as powerfully to the failures of the left today as it did thirty years ago. *Out of Apathy*, the first book produced by the New Left, was devoted to this theme, and it is for this reason that we have appropriated the title for this book.

In their essays on socialist humanism, Thompson and others emphasized the creative potential of individuals. They argued that men and women create not only themselves as individuals but also their collective lives – their societies, their political realities, their history. They asserted that a humanist socialism must seek to liberate men and women as creative, moral beings; that socialism should above all increase our capacity, individually and collectively, to shape our lives according to fundamental human values and ideas. If politics ought to reflect these values, they argued, then utopian thinking must be given a central place. If apathy was to be overcome, then images of society must be promoted which would inspire popular support and confront the enervating ideology of instrumental necessity and political expediency. While New Left writers were highly critical of the elitism of vanguardist and Fabian models of intellectual leadership, they did regard intellectuals as having a leading role in formulating alternative visions of a socialist future and in testing them against the real desires of actual people. As Thompson explained:

> the value of utopianism is to be found, not in raising banners in the wilderness, but in confronting living people with an image of their own potential life, in summoning up their aspirations so that they challenge the old forms of life, and in influencing such social choices as there are in the direction that is desired. (*ULR* 6)

Elsewhere he declared: 'we continue our intellectual work because we believe that . . . *ideas matter*'; and he went on to argue that committed intellectuals 'must leap the gap that divides ideas from social energies. And this means, in the last analysis, opening new circuits between the "intellectual" and the people' (*ULR* 1).

Many of the themes and commitments which were given philosophical expression in this conception of socialist humanism also emerged in the New Left's distinctive development of a cultural politics. The early writings of Richard Hoggart and Raymond Williams had a particularly forceful impact on the early New Left's thinking, initiating a debate about culture as the sphere in which social meanings and values are generated. Like its writing about socialist humanism, the New Left's theorizing about culture reasserted the creativity of individuals and the way in which society, politics and history are produced by individuals in a constant creative engagement with their social and cultural inheritance. Williams and others emphasized the totality of the various spheres of human existence: that art and politics are not separate from ordinary life but are, rather, parts of a vast web of collectively defined human relations and commonly created meanings. This web – 'a whole way of life' – constitutes our culture, in the broadest sense of the word. Art and politics, social and economic life, the private and the public, are all embedded in this web of culture, interdependent, mutually influencing and transforming one another.

This view of culture as a whole way of life led to a distinctive and radical expansion of the New Left's conception of politics. One of the most exciting features of the early New Left's project was the attempt to break down the barriers between politics, art and everyday life. In reaction to the Stalinist abuses of culture, the independent post-war left had generally retreated from the attempt to relate social and cultural life to questions of political commitment. Writers in the New Left journals, employing a much more sensitive and unorthodox analysis, began once again to explore the political significance of many of these 'non-political' subjects such as literature, art, 'personal' experience. In the New Left clubs and in the journals, debates took place about the meaning of political commitment in the arts and in art criticism. Artists and critics of many sorts were drawn into the movement.

But the New Left did not merely politicize art; it sought to expand and humanize politics itself. A whole range of 'quality of life' issues were added to the political agenda: articles appeared in the journals not only about literature, theatre and cinema but also about town planning, modern architecture, social alienation, and youth subcultures. 'When socialist values lose their relevance for the total scale of man's [sic] activities,' explained the editorial of the first issue of ULR, 'they lose their "political" point as well.' Williams declared that 'culture is ordinary', and the New Left affirmed with him that politics and art – like all other forms of social behaviour – must have a common human reference. Politics, like art, was not viewed as a project of identifying inexorable laws which determined the lives of individuals; rather, both were regarded as part of the constant collective process through which men and women create their common culture, inventing and extending the meanings of their lives. Cultural criticism and cultural construction, in art and in everyday life, came to be understood as intrinsic parts of an extended political process of defining values and shaping society.

The early New Left spelled out the radical implications of this comprehensive cultural conception: because we constantly re-create the whole of our culture, including social and political arrangements, we should be able to make this process of collective creation a conscious and moral one. Williams and others argued for a radical democratic transformation of the construction of our common life. This vision shares the same basic moral intuition as that which impels the ideal of socialist humanism: the belief that 'the moral imagination can still intervene creatively in human history' (ULR 1); that our social and political world is a collective creation, and that socialism ought to involve a democratic transformation of this process. The editors of ULR thus asserted as the goal of the new movement 'the creation of a genuinely democratic way of life'.

While the early New Left often conceived of itself as a 'movement of ideas', this never implied a separation of theory and practice. Rather, its theorizing emerged from an analysis of political realities, and its writings were linked to a fundamental desire to shape policy and to build a political movement. Across a wide range of practical campaigns, the same basic moral considerations – the concern for democratic control and self-determination, the emphasis on the importance of moral values in political decisions, and the liberation of individual creative energies – seem to have shaped the movement's political agenda.

In the international sphere, the New Left's commitment to democratic self-determination was clearly manifested in its resistance to the Cold War and its advocacy of a foreign policy of 'positive neutralism'. As Suez and Hungary had demonstrated, genuine self-rule for countries around the globe required an end to bloc politics and to superpower intervention. The New Left argued that Britain should join the newly independent nations of the decolonizing 'Third World' in declaring itself non-aligned from both superpower blocs. The movement's proposed policy of positive neutralism called for the establishment of constructive economic and political relations with all non-aligned nations, in order to create a secure base for independent development and self-rule. New Left foreign policy did not seek to dictate a particular course of economic or political development to the new post-colonial nations, but rather to create a kind of global third space in which the peoples of all parts of the world could search freely for their own paths of social development.

Resisting the Cold War also meant resisting the bomb, and the New Left actively supported the Campaign for Nuclear Disarmament (CND). The nuclear arms race represented to the New Left the ultimate betrayal of humanist values in which social democratic and conservative, capitalist and officially Communist governments all seemed equally willing to participate. The campaign against the bomb became for many an embodiment of the socialist humanist impulse: the attempt to exercise rational and moral control over our own social creations; to engage in moral protest against an ideology of passivity which leads blindly to self-destruction. In this spirit, for example, Edward Thompson described CND as an 'assault against fatalism' which 'opposes a categorical moral imperative to all the life-corrupting arguments of expediency' (*The New Reasoner* 5). New Left activists played a central role in organizing the first Aldermaston marches, which marked the emergence of CND as a mass movement. It was in fact the association with CND which gave the

New Left more of the character of a large-scale social movement.

In the domestic sphere, the New Left's practical policy initiatives also reflected its commitment to the creation of a more participatory, more truly democratic society. Although members shared the basic faith of the post-war left in economic planning, they nevertheless initiated a tentative critique of the dangers of centralized control. In several areas they argued for a shift in economic policy away from bureaucratic forms of planning towards a greater degree of workers' control. John Hughes and Ken Alexander, for example, in the New Left pamphlet *A Socialist Wages Plan*, outlined a strategy for working people and the labour movement to take control of economic growth and inflation through voluntary restraints on wage demands. Such a wages plan, if implemented by the Labour Party and the trade unions, would, they hoped, help to shift primary control of the economy from the bureaucrats at the Treasury in Whitehall and put it instead in the hands of ordinary men and women. In a similar fashion, the New Left initiated a critique of the Morrisonian model of nationalization and championed the cause of workers' self-management. As a first step towards a greater degree of workers' control of industry they advocated worker representation on the boards of public enterprises to reduce the control of civil servants and private-sector capitalists.

The New Left thus sought to construct a socialist and democratic agenda that would address, from a radical humanist position, a wide range of economic, political and cultural issues. In this book, a number of elements of that agenda are defended and redefined by some of the people who helped to formulate them. John Hughes, Michael Barratt Brown and Peter Worsley all argue for the continued relevance of specific New Left economic and foreign-policy initiatives, while they also indicate where the original analyses went wrong and why the movement failed ultimately to gain broader political support for these ideas.

Perhaps the largest critical question that emerges from this collection, raised by a number of contributions from various perspectives, concerns the contrast between the early New Left's intellectual and cultural vitality on the one hand, and its relative political weakness on the other. The New Left conceived of itself as 'a movement of ideas', and at the level of ideas few would deny the sustained influence which the movement has exerted not only on the British left but also, via various later movements and appropriations, on New Left political formations in many other countries. Michael Rustin argues in his chapter that the New Left has successfully created a 'radical culture' in Britain that has established a vital minority presence throughout academia and the educational system, and across the arts, from architecture to the natural sciences, from the cinema to journalism.

But the New Left did not conceive of itself as simply an intellectual movement. As Stuart Hall suggests in his opening chapter, the New Left was struggling to establish itself as a new kind of political entity – as a 'movement of ideas' which would provide the focus for various kinds of political mobilization; as a genuinely popular movement which would not be trapped within the Labour Party but would exercise powerful influence on it; as a movement which could work closely with the emerging peace movement, and develop its socialist implications.

The New Left came into being when the first post-war social movements were emerging. In its early days the movement began the process of trying to define the forms and strategies for a truly popular and democratic, radical politics which could work with political parties as the vehicles for implementing policy, but would remain free from the rigidities of institutionalized party practice. Stuart Hall argues that the early New Left did succeed in expanding the definition and the practice of politics, in identifying important new sites of political resistance and new constituencies and agents for social change beyond the labour movement. He suggests, however, that it did ultimately fail, as later formations on the left have failed, to bring together the heterogeneous groups and movements which constituted this expanded politics into an effective political bloc or coalition. Similarly, Michael Rustin argues that the New Left's political weaknesses stemmed from its limited social base in a 'class of cultural workers' and its inability to build political bridges to the labour movement and other constituencies of the left. 'A political movement was therefore what the early New Left wanted to be, not what it was', he concludes.

While many of the contributors to this book would probably agree with Rustin's conclusion, most also seem convinced that the kind of movement the New Left wanted to be remains in many respects an appropriate aspiration for the left. The expanded and diversified conception of politics which the early New Left began to formulate remains for many of us, across political generations and nationalities, a basis for any relevant left politics. The difficulty of building a politics based on a recognition of the diversities of constituency and experience that are present in our societies is evident to all. Some of these difficulties, intellectual and strategic, are raised in the final chapter of this book. Charles Taylor argues for the need to abandon a unified and monolithic conception of an 'a priori socialism' that will address all the concerns of the left at once and abolish all social conflict. Stuart Hall discusses the problem in terms of constructing a radical politics 'rooted in a recognition of differences'. Raphael Samuel speaks of the need to discover a 'majoritarian language' in which to articulate a common politics composed of many diverse – and often minority – causes.

Some of the voices which spoke from the margins of the 'Out of Apathy' conference – the voices of feminists and ecology activists – raised questions about the gaps in the New Left agenda and underlined further the importance of incorporating new issues and new voices into a relevant politics of the left today. Other voices, from other minorities with different causes, will of course demand yet other requirements and sensitivities from the left in the late 1980s and 1990s. The fact that the first New Left did not answer the question of how to build an effective movement to incorporate these diverse politics, and how to relate them to the politics of class, should not come as a surprise.

The New Left of the 1950s began an important project of renewal. Their candour and innovation command respect. The affirmation of a radical humanism, the questioning of orthodoxy, the expansion of the definition of politics – these are some of the seeds from which a renewed left politics must grow. Their project was, of course, far from perfect, far from complete. The political space which they pioneered proved too narrow or too distant to include important emerging constituencies. This independent space still urgently awaits its definition, its programme and its strategies. We must not fault them for failing to do in the 1950s what we have yet to succeed at in the 1980s. The task of renewal remains, as always, unfinished; remains before us.

Seth Moglen
Oxford November 1988

1

The 'First' New Left: Life and Times

Stuart Hall

In his interpretative history of the 'first' New Left, Stuart Hall combines a sketch of his own background with a picture of the broader context from which the New Left emerged, and of its intellectual concerns and activities. He emphasizes, in particular, its attempt to assess the significance of the social and political changes in post-war capitalism. The developing 'sense of classlessness' required a new, 'populist' politics, grounded in the experiences and concerns of ordinary people. In its cultural analysis and in its interest in movement politics, Hall concludes, the New Left prefigured later developments in socialist theory and practice.

For Alan Hall

The 'first' New Left was born in '1956', a conjuncture (not just a year) bounded on one side by the suppression of the Hungarian Revolution by Soviet tanks in November and on the other by the British and French invasion of the Suez Canal zone. These two events, whose dramatic impact was heightened by the fact that they occurred within days of each other, unmasked the underlying violence and aggression latent in the two systems which dominated political life at that time – Western imperialism and Stalinism – and sent a shock wave through the political world. In a deeper sense, they defined for people of my generation the boundaries and limits of the tolerable in politics. Socialists after 'Hungary', it seemed to us, must carry in their hearts the sense of tragedy which the degeneration of the Russian Revolution into Stalinism represents for the left in the twentieth century. 'Hungary' brought to an end a certain kind of socialist 'innocence'. On the other hand, 'Suez' underlined the enormity of the error in believing that lowering the Union Jack in a few ex-colonies necessarily signalled the 'end of imperialism' or that the real gains of the welfare state and the widening of material affluence meant the end of inequality and exploitation. 'Hungary' and 'Suez' were thus 'liminal', boundary-marking experiences. They symbolized the break-up of the political Ice Age.

The New Left came into existence in the aftermath of these two events. It attempted to define a 'third' political space somewhere between these two metaphors. Its rise signified for people on the left in my generation the end of the tyranny, the imposed silences and political impasses, of the Cold War in politics, and the possibility of a break-through into a new socialist project.

There are two main purposes in writing, now, about the life and times of the 'first' New Left. First, to set out, from the point of view of one

13

who participated in it, how it happened – its early formation and project – before the details disappear from memory or the yellowing files are consigned to what Engels once called 'the gnawing criticism of the mice'. The 'first' New Left is once again exciting interest amongst younger people (the Oxford conference being one manifestation of this) – principally because of certain perceived parallels between the 1950s and early 1960s and the difficult times which the left has been experiencing in the 1980s. I am sure such parallels can be instructive, but they need to be firmly contextualized in the climate and 'structure of feeling' of their times.

What people seem to 'know' nowadays about the '1956 New Left' mainly concerns how *New Left Review* passed from the hands of the 'first' into the keeping of the very different 'second' generation. This is, without doubt, a riveting story, much enlarged and distorted by rumour and counter-rumour, about which several of the key participants in the drama (Edward Thompson, Perry Anderson, Raymond Williams) have written vivid, if not wholly consistent, accounts. However, this aspect is now in danger of skewing a more general interest in the topic.

The second purpose is more personal: to situate my own politics in relation to that formative experience and, in doing so, to honour the friendship and memory of Alan Hall, with whom I shared much of those times. I first met Alan when he came to Balliol in 1952 from Aberdeen. He subsequently lectured in classics at Keele and was a passionate archaeologist of Graeco-Roman remains in Anatolia. He played a key role in the early New Left (including the passage from first to second generation) but died, tragically, in his fifties before he had the opportunity to put the New Left story on record himself.

Such an account makes no claim to be neutral, since it is written from the viewpoint of a participant rather than an objective chronicler, with all the selectivity of interpretation which the former implies. Others who were just as actively involved, but had different pathways through – and in some cases out of – the New Left, could (and will in time) tell a different, though no less valid, story. Meanwhile, this brief 'memoir' is fated to mix history with memory and desire – a combination which future historians will treat with due suspicion.

It is useful to begin with genealogy. The term 'New Left' is commonly associated these days with '1968', but to the '1956' New Left generation, '1968' was already a second, even perhaps a third, 'mutation'. We had borrowed the phrase in the 1950s from the movement known as the *'nouvelle gauche'*, an independent tendency in French politics associated with the weekly newspaper *France Observateur* and its editor, Claude Bourdet. Bourdet, a leading figure in the French Resistance, personified the attempt, after the war, to open a 'third way' in European politics, independent of the two dominant left positions of Stalinism and social democracy, 'beyond' the military power blocs of NATO and the Warsaw Pact, and opposed to both the American and Soviet presences in Europe. This 'third position' paralleled the political aspirations of many of the people who came together to form the early British New Left.

Some of us, including Alan Hall, first met Claude Bourdet in Paris, at a conference called to consider setting up an International Socialist Society, across the divisions between Western and Eastern Europe. The main protagonist of the idea in Britain was G.D.H. Cole, an austere and courageous veteran of the independent left, who was at that time still teaching politics at Oxford. Although he was a distinguished historian of European socialism and a student of Marxism, Cole's socialism was rooted in the co-operativist and 'workers' control' traditions of Guild Socialism. He was the first socialist whom I ever heard advance, from the basis of a more democratic conception of social ownership, a full-scale critique of the bureaucratic forms of 'Morrisonian'-style national-ization favoured by the 1945 Labour government. This critique has been enormously influential in shaping the attitude of many socialists of my generation towards 'statist' forms of socialism.

The New Left represented the coming together of two related but different traditions – also of two political experiences or 'generations'. One was the tradition I would call, for want of a better term, communist humanism, symbolized by *The New Reasoner* and its founders, John Saville and Dorothy and Edward Thompson. The second is perhaps best described as an 'independent socialist' tradition. Many of the people in this second group were influenced by Marxism and some were, for a time, Communists (Raphael Samuel has re-created this political milieu in 'The Lost World of British Communism' (*NLR* 154). Nevertheless the majority were not, and its centre of gravity, in my reading, lay in that left student generation of the 1950s which maintained some distance from 'party' affiliations and, in the disintegration of those orthodoxies in '1956', first produced *Universities and Left Review*. I belong to this second tradition. I shall try, first, to re-create the circumstances out of which this New Left tendency arose.

It may help to understand that moment better if I speak personally. I arrived in Oxford on a Rhodes scholarship, more or less straight from school in Jamaica, in 1951. I would say that my politics were principally 'anti-imperialist'. I was sympathetic to the left, had read Marx and been influenced by him while at school, but I would not, at the time, have called myself a Marxist in the European sense. In any event, I was troubled by the failure of orthodox Marxism to deal adequately with either 'Third World' issues of race and ethnicity or with the questions of racism or of literature and culture which preoccupied me intellectually as an undergraduate. Retrospectively, I would identify myself as one of those described by Raymond Williams in *Culture and Society* who, following, as a student of literature, the engagement between the Leavisites and the Marxist critics, was obliged to acknowledge that '*Scrutiny* won' – not because it was right (we were always critical of the conservative elitism of *Scrutiny*'s cultural programme) but because the alternative Marxist models were far too mechanical and reductive. (We did not yet have access to Lukács, Benjamin, Gramsci or Adorno.) On the wider political front, I was strongly critical of everything I knew about Stalinism, either as a political system or as a form of politics. I opposed it as a model for a democratic socialism and could not fathom the reluctance of the few Communists I met to acknowledge the truth of what was by then common knowledge about its disastrous consequences for Soviet society and Eastern Europe.

Like the rest of the small number of 'Third World' students at Oxford, my principal political concerns were with 'colonial' questions. I became very involved in West Indian student politics. We debated and discussed, mainly, what was going on 'back home' in the expectation that before long we would all be there and involved in it; we argued about the West Indian Federation and the prospects for a new Carib-bean economic order, the expulsion of the left from Manley's PNP Party in Jamaica under the pressures of the Cold War, the overthrow of the Jagan government in British Guyana with the suspension of the consti-tution and the moving in of British troops. There was no 'black politics' in Britain; post-war migration had only just begun. Later, as I began to take a wider interest in British politics, I came more into contact with the 'Oxford left'. There was no 'mass' British political movement of the left or major popular political issue to which one could attach oneself. The choice seemed to be between a Labour Party which, at that moment, was deeply committed to an Atlanticist world-view, and the outer dark-ness of the 'far left'. The first time I ventured into a Communist Group discussion meeting was to debate with the CP the application of Marx's concept of class to contemporary capitalist society. At the time, I felt that this was an extremely bold move – such was the climate of fear and suspicion which prevailed.

After 1954, this climate began to change. There was a slow, hesitant revival of debate on the left and a group began to emerge around these discussions. Many of us attended the 'Cole Group' (as his seminar in politics was known), which, though formally an occasion for graduate students, doubled up as a wide-ranging discussion group of the broad left. Some of the earliest contacts and friendships, which were later to be cemented by the formation of the New Left, were first forged there. The student house where a number of us lived, in Richmond Road (in the old Jewish quarter, 'Jericho', behind Ruskin College), was another, more informal focal point of these discussions.

It is difficult, now, to conjure up the political climate of Oxford in the 1950s. Even for people like Alan Hall and myself, who debated political and theoretical questions with Communists but never had any intention of joining the Party, the 'Cold War' dominated the political horizon, positioning everyone and polarizing every topic by its remorseless binary logic. Its atmosphere was accurately caught in the first *ULR* editorial:

> The post-war decade was one in which declining political orthodoxies held sway. Every political concept became a weapon in the cold war of ideas, every idea had its label, every person had his [*sic*] place in the political spectrum, every form of political action appeared – in someone's eyes – a polite treason. To recommend the admission of China to the UN was to invite the opprobrium of 'fellow-traveller'; to say that the character of contemporary capitalism had changed was to be ranked as a 'Keynesian liberal'. Between the high citadel of Stalinist Russia and the 'welfare state – no further' jungle of the mixed economy, there seemed nothing but an arid waste. [Caught between] these tightly compartmentalized worlds . . . British socialism suffered a moral and intellectual eclipse. . . . Nevertheless, the age of orthodoxies has once again been outstripped by historical events. . . . The thaw is on . . .

This 'thaw' began as a slow, hesitant debate about a range of contemporary issues: the future of Labour and the left in the wake of the Conservative revival; the nature of the welfare state and post-war capitalism; the impact of cultural change on British society in the early 'affluent' years of the decade. The pace of this debate was accelerated by the Khrushchev revelations at the Twentieth Congress of the CPSU. The response to '1956' and the formation of a New Left could not have occurred without this prior period of 'preparation', in which a number of people slowly gained the confidence to engage in a dialogue which questioned the terms of the orthodox political argument and cut across existing organizational boundaries. Just as a way of characterizing the range of this debate, Alan Hall and I spent the summer before Suez and Hungary trying to sketch out a book on the new contours of cultural change in 'Contemporary Capitalism' which would reflect this debate. We took away with us, among many other books, the following key texts: Crosland's *Future of Socialism*; Strachey's *End of Empire*; two chapters of what was to become Raymond Williams's *Culture and Society*; F.R. Leavis's *Culture and Environment*; Angus Maude's smug little book on *The English Middle Classes*; Osborne's *Look Back In Anger* and George Scott's 'angry young man's' autobiography, *Time And Place*.

Whether we knew it or not, we were struggling with a difficult act of description, trying to find a language in which to map an emergent 'new world' and its cultural transformations, which defied analysis within the conventional terms of the left while at the same time deeply undermining them. These reference points had all emerged in the discussion in the left circles we inhabited in the two years before Suez. The issue of the Oxford Labour Club magazine, *Clarion*, which our group edited in summer 1957, presented as its central political document a discussion of Richard Hoggart's *Uses of Literacy*. Noting that we had been criticized by both the orthodox Labourist wing and the student organizer of the CP for not having enough about politics and being too preoccupied with 'new and novel definitions', we replied that

> confusion and uncertainty are the perils of rethinking . . . we may appear, for a time, to have left behind 'serious thoughts about the next Labour government'. But if it is true that 'the bottom has fallen out of politics' . . . we must discover where it lies. You cannot construct a political programme over a vacuum.

Plus ça change. . . . These strands were dramatically condensed by the events of '1956'. Soviet tanks in Budapest terminated any hope that a more human and democratic brand of communism would evolve in Eastern Europe without prolonged trauma and social convulsion. Suez punctured the cosy illusion that (to adapt Tawney's phrase) 'you could skin the capitalist–imperialist tiger stripe by stripe'. The Trafalgar Square Suez demonstration was the first mass political rally of its kind in the 1950s, and the first time I encountered police horses face to face, or heard Hugh Gaitskell and Nye Bevan speak in public. Bevan's fierce denunciation of Eden, I remember, scattered the startled pigeons into flight. . . . One outcome of the ferment of '1956' was the publication of the two journals, *Universities and Left Review* and *The New Reasoner*, which, when they subsequently merged (in 1960), formed the 'first' *New Left Review*.

How and why did this happen then – and why, of all places, partly in Oxford? In the 1950s universities were not, as they later became, centres of revolutionary activity. A minority of privileged left-wing students, debating consumer capitalism and the embourgeoisement of working-class culture amidst the 'dreaming spires', may seem, in retrospect, a pretty marginal political phenomenon. Nevertheless, the debate was joined with a fierce intensity, self-consciously counterposed to the brittle, casual self-confidence of Oxford's dominant tone. (Few people understand that what appealed to those of us reading English about *Scrutiny* was not its cultural conservatism but its 'moral seriousness', as contrasted with Oxford's willed triviality).

Outsiders like myself found it particularly hard to adjust to being catapulted into the centre of the process by which the English class system reproduced itself, educationally and culturally. The Oxford of the mid 1950s was dominated by the 'Hooray Henries' of its time, attempting to relive *Brideshead Revisited*. Its atmosphere was relentlessly masculine, and – though we did not recognize it at the time – sexist. I 'hear' that Oxford now principally as a particular pitch of the voice – the upper-middle-class English male commanding attention to confidently expressed banalities as a sort of seigneurial right. . . . In fact, Oxford also contained its rebel enclaves: demobbed young veterans and national servicemen, Ruskin College trade unionists, 'scholarship boys' and girls from home and abroad. Although they were unable to redefine its dominant culture, these outsiders did come to constitute an alternative – not to say beleaguered – intellectual minority culture. This was the '*ULR* constituency'.

The Oxford left was very diverse. There was a small number of CP members – including Raphael Samuel, Peter Sedgwick, Gabriel Pearson – mainly in Balliol, where Christopher Hill was the tutor in modern history. They were somewhat embattled because of their association with an unpopular and, in Cold War terms, 'subversive' organization – although actually they knew and were known and liked by 'everybody' in Oxford at the time. This, after all, was still the era of 'bans and proscriptions', when Communists were forbidden to take part in any Labour Party activity, when the CIA and *Encounter* policed the intellectual frontiers. It sometimes seemed as if to be seen talking to 'the Balliol Reds' put one in danger of falling off the edge of the 'civilized world' straight into the Siberian labour camps.

Next, there was the great body of 'Labour Club' supporters, the majority firmly attached to Fabian, Labourist and reformist positions, and a few with their eyes fixed unswervingly on their coming parliamentary careers. (Several later became Labour and SDP household names. One of their number, a prominent right-wing Labour MP before his very public – but to those of us who knew him, not at all surprising – conversion to 'Thatcherism', once told me: 'The Labour Party is not for the likes of you' . . .) Finally there were a small number of 'independents', including some serious Labour people, intellectually aligned with neither of these two camps, who shuttled somewhat uneasily between them.

The latter group attracted more than its fair share of exiles and migrants, which reinforced its cosmopolitanism. 'Chuck' Taylor was a French-Canadian Rhodes scholar (as well as that even more perplexing phenomenon, a sort of Catholic Marxist); Dodd Alleyne was Trinidadian;

I was Jamaican, Sadiq al Mahdi was later to play a significant role
in the Sudan; Clovis Maksoud was a founder member of the Syrian
Ba'ath Party. Some, like Alan Lovell, a Welsh pacifist and conscientious
objector, Alan Hall, a Scots classicist from Aberdeen, and Raphael
Samuel, Gabriel Pearson, Stanley Mitchell and Robert Cassen, who
were all Jewish, were what one might call 'internal émigrés'; though, to
be fair, others, like Anna Davin, Luke Hodgkin, Rod Prince, David
Marquand, David and Michael Armstrong, even Perry Anderson
(despite the Irish connection), seemed to our unpractised eye
unquestionably, even luminously, 'English'.

The locus of our debate was the Socialist Club, a moribund organization left more or less abandoned since its thirties 'Popular Front'
days, which we resuscitated. It became clear that similar debates were
developing in other universities and that there ought to be some
common platform for this emerging student 'left'. This explains the word
'Universities' in the title of the journal we eventually produced. The
other half of its cumbersome and extremely uncommercial title signalled
our concern with cultural questions, via a symbolic link with *The Left
Review*, a wide-ranging and unorthodox literary and cultural journal of
the 1930s and 1940s, more receptive to new cultural movements (for
example, in its openness to 'Modernist' currents) than any comparable
'party' journal of its time. (Raymond Williams, in *Politics and Letters*,
reminds us that Brecht was first published in England in its pages.)
1956, however, destroyed the student-bound confines of this debate and
catapulted us into the maelstrom of national and international left
politics. The contents of and contributors to *ULR* 1 – Isaac Deutscher,
Bourdet, Lindsay Anderson, E.P. Thompson, Cole, Hobsbawm, Graeme
Shankland on town planning, David Marquand on *Lucky Jim*, Joan Robin-
son, Basil Davidson – clearly demonstrate this translation to a wider stage.

The first issue of *ULR*, which appeared in spring 1957, had four
editors: Raphael Samuel and Gabriel Pearson, who left the CP after
Hungary, and Charles Taylor and myself, representing 'the independents'. Too much should not be made of those particular names
since, out of the ferment, almost any four people would have done. We
were, in a sense, the group's 'informal representatives'; but many others
helped to launch the journal and kept it going. Had the concept been
available to us, we would have said that we all belonged to the '*ULR*
collective', which for a time convened nightly in the student house in
Richmond Road where a number of us lived.

The Oxford part is, of course, only half the story. The New Left had
equally important, though very different, roots in another tradition,
represented by *The New Reasoner*. This tendency had a quite different
formation in Communist and Popular Front politics in Britain. Some of

the 'Reasoners' (E.P. Thompson, J. Saville, R. Hilton, C. Hill, V. Kiernan, E. Hobsbawm) had belonged to that unique enclave inside the Party's Historians' Group which, under the inspiration of the little-known Dona Torr, developed a highly independent and original 'reading' of British history, and a form of Marxist politics much more in touch with English popular radicalism and quite distinct in style and inspiration from that sustained in the CP leadership by powerful but deeply sectarian figures like Palme Dutt.

The revelations of the Twentieth Congress stimulated inside the Party a painful reassessment of the whole Stalinist experience and *The Reasoner* first appeared, in this context, as an internal opposition bulletin insisting on an open and public 'calling to accounts'. It was only after they lost their struggle for the right to express what were officially defined as 'factional' opinions, and the disciplines of democratic centralism were mobilized against them, that the majority of the 'Reasoners' either left the Party or were expelled and *The New Reasoner* appeared as an independent journal of the left. The final issue of *The Reasoner* was planned and produced before Suez and Hungary but, for it, these events were 'epochal':

> Even the urgency of the Egyptian crisis cannot disguise the fact that the events of Budapest represent a crucial turning-point for our Party. The aggression of British imperialism is uglier and more cynical than previous imperialist aggressions. But the crisis in world Communism is now different in kind.

In the aftermath of Hungary large numbers of people left the Communist Party, and *The New Reasoner* and subsequently the New Left provided some of them with a political rallying point without which many would doubtless have abandoned politics for good.

The New Left therefore represented the coming together of two different political traditions. How did this occur, and how well did it work? The organizational details of the amalgamation between the two journals can be quickly summarized. They continued to publish in tandem for a while, advertising and promoting each other. After a time the two editorial boards began to meet regularly around a broader political agenda, to appoint editorial board members in common and to recruit new ones, like John Rex, Peter Worsley, Alasdair MacIntyre, Norman Birnbaum, Michael Barratt Brown, Ralph Miliband, Paddy Whannel and Raymond Williams, who did not originally belong to either.

Both boards were increasingly preoccupied with the struggle to sustain the financial and commercial viability of two journals. Even more pressing was the cost in human capital. For many of us, normal life had more or less been suspended in 1956. Some had not stopped running round in circles since – to borrow Lady Eden's graphic phrase – 'the Suez Canal flowed through the drawing room', and were by then in a state of extreme political exhaustion. There were also, more positively, the opportunities we were missing to create a much wider, united political platform for our position. While we were aware of our differences, our perspectives had come closer together in the months of collaboration. Out of this variety of factors came the decision to merge and, with more suitable candidates like E.P. Thompson and others being unwilling to serve, I rashly agreed to become the first editor of *New Left Review*, with John Saville acting as chairman of the editorial board.

New Left Review in this form lasted two years. It was never, I think, as successful or distinctive a journal as either of its predecessors – a failure which clearly reflected my own editorial inexperience. The bimonthly rhythm and the pressures to connect with immediate political issues pushed us into becoming more of a left 'magazine' than a 'journal'. This required a shift of journalistic and editorial style which did not square with the original political intention and for which the board was unprepared. There were differences of emphasis and style of work between the board, which carried the main political weight and authority of the movement, and the small working editorial group that began to assemble around Carlisle Street. The latter included people like Norm Fruchter, later a founding figure in the American 'New Left', and some of the younger 'New Left' group in Oxford. The latter had followed the original *ULR* generation and produced their own journal, *New University* – the route by which Perry Anderson, Robin Blackburn, Mike Rustin, Gareth Stedman Jones, Alan Shuttleworth and many others first became latched into the New Left.

The 'New Reasoners' – Edward and Dorothy Thompson, John Saville, and others on the *Reasoner* board like Ronald Meek, Ken Alexander, Doris Lessing – belonged to a political generation formed by the politics of the Popular Front and the anti-Fascist movements of the thirties, the European Resistance movements during the war, the 'Second Front' campaigns for 'friendship with the Soviet Union' and the popular turn to the left reflected in the 1945 Labour victory. Although some younger Communists in the *ULR* tendency also belonged to this tradition, their relation to it was always different. In its overwhelming majority, the *ULR* generation's centre of gravity was irrevocably 'post-war'. This was a difference not of age but of formation – a question of *political generations*, within which the war constituted the symbolic dividing line. These differences did produce subtle tensions which surfaced around the new journal. Later, when things began to fall apart, some people, who had never much favoured merger in the first place, argued that with hindsight the two formations did better when they were free to do their own distinctive thing, and that the 'marriage' was a misalliance. I do not subscribe to that view. Nevertheless, although these differences never threatened our underlying solidarities and sense of common purpose, they made close working collaboration difficult at times.

These differences of formation and political style of work were magnified by the location of the two tendencies in two quite distinct social and cultural milieux. *The New Reasoner*'s base was in Yorkshire and the industrial North. Although it had many readers elsewhere, it was organically rooted in a provincial political culture – not just that of the labour movement but also of organizations like the Yorkshire Peace Committee – and was intensely suspicious of 'London'. *ULR* also attracted support from many parts of the country; but it very much belonged to what the 'Reasoners' thought of as the 'cosmopolitan' or 'Oxford/London' axis. Although we did not consciously understand it at the time, the 'ULR-ers' were 'Modernists', if not actually 'rootless cosmopolitans'. As a colonial, I certainly felt instinctively more at home in the more socially anonymous metropolitan culture, though I regretted *ULR*'s lack of organic connections to non-metropolitan working-class life.

It should by now be clear that even within the editorial boards of the original journals, the New Left was far from politically monolithic and certainly never became culturally or politically homogeneous. The tensions were, for the most part, humanely and generously handled. But any careful reader of the different journals will quickly be able to identify real points of difference and, on occasion, fiercely contended debates surfacing in their pages. It would therefore be quite wrong to attempt to reconstruct, retrospectively, some essential 'New Left', and to impose on it a political unity it never possessed. Nevertheless, although no two members would offer the same list, there was a set of linked themes – a 'thematics', if you like – which commanded wide enough assent to make it distinctive as a political formation.

In my reading, this centred on the argument that any prospect for the renewal of the left had to begin with a new conception of socialism and a radically new analysis of the social relations, dynamics and culture of post-war capitalism. Far from constituting a modest updating exercise, this was a far-reaching, ambitious and multifaceted intellectual project. So far as socialism was concerned, it meant coming to terms with the depressing experiences of both 'actual existing socialism' and 'actual existing social democracy' and transforming, in the light of those experiences, the very conception of 'the political'. So far as the latter was

concerned, what we called modern 'corporate capitalism' had very
different economic, organizational, social and cultural forms. It func-
tioned according to a different 'logic' from that of entrepreneurial capitalism, described in Marx's classic theses or embedded in the language
and theory of the left and inscribed in its agendas, its institutions and its
revolutionary scenarios. For many of us (though not for everyone) this
struggle to ground socialism in a new analysis of 'our times' was primary
and originating – where the whole New Left project began. This was
both a theoretical and a political question, since from the mid 1950s
onwards, Labour – having lost the 1951 and 1955, and shortly thereafter the 1959, elections – started to tear itself apart in the first post-war
'revisionist' debate which had these questions at its centre.

The dominant account offered was that we were entering a 'post-
capitalist' society in which the principal problems of social distribution
had been solved by the post-war boom coupled to the expansion of the
welfare state, Keynesian macroeconomic regulation and the 'human
face' of the managerial revolution. All these were elements of what later
came to be known as 'corporatism' – big capital, big state – or, from
another point of view, the 'post-war consensus'. They had led to an
erosion of traditional class cultures and the 'embourgeoisement' of the
working class. Around the corner lay 'Mr Crosland's Dreamland' which
Perry Anderson identified, in an arresting article in *NLR*, with Sweden –
which most of us thought of more as an 'Americanized' Britain:
hamburger stores at every intersection, and the open, unfenced reaches
of new-town suburbia stretching into infinity: rather like Thatcherite
Britain, as it turned out. However, the scenario differed from Thatcherism in at least this respect: Britain, it was said, would cross the threshold
into this modern 'utopia' effortlessly and painlessly.

Opposed to this scenario was the 'Old Left' argument that since the
system was still patently capitalist, nothing of any significance had
changed. The classes and the class struggle were exactly what and where
they had always been, and to question this was to betray the revolutionary cause. The majority of the New Left, however, refused this binary
logic, arguing that post-war capitalism *had* changed. The new forms of
property, corporate organization and the dynamics of modern accumu-
lation and consumption required a new analysis. These processes had
had effects on social structure and political consciousness. More
broadly, the spread of consumerism had disarticulated many traditional
cultural attitudes and social hierarchies, and this had consequences for
politics, the constituencies for change and the institutions and agendas
of the left, with which socialism must come to terms. Lacking much
indigenous material to go on, the American analysts – Riesman,
Galbraith, Wright Mills – who were at the cutting edge of these develop-

ments provided us with our main purchase on these arguments.

Closely linked to this was the argument about the contradictory and politically indeterminate 'drift' of social and cultural change. These changes fell short of a transformation of society, yet clearly but ambiguously dismantled many of the old relations and formations on which the whole edifice of the left and the project of socialism had historically been constructed. Again, there were at least two competing versions of this. One was that since the fundamental class structure of British society remained intact, 'change' could be only of the most superficial 'sociological' kind. It picked up incidental and mainly stylistic differences in such marginal areas as new attitudes and life-styles amongst young people, new patterns of urban life, the movement out of the inner cities, the growing importance of consumption in everyday life, the 'weakening' of older social identities, and so on, which did not touch 'the fundamentals'. This fundamentalist account was matched, on the other side, by a relentless celebration of change for its own sake in which the new mass media had acquired a massive investment. With the expansion of the new journalism, the spread of mass culture and the rise of commercial television, society seemed bewitched by images of itself in motion, reflecting off its shiny consumer surfaces. Life was increasingly described here in the mindlessly trendy imagery of the absolute divide between 'then' – that is, 'before the war' – and 'now', after free orange juice, school meals, the Labour government and *Rock Around the Clock* . . .

Again, the New Left insisted on occupying neither of these simple alternatives, choosing instead a more complex 'third' description. We were not necessarily at one in terms of how we understood these shifts (the debate between Edward Thompson, Raphael Samuel and myself on my speculative piece, 'A Sense of Classlessness', in the pages of *ULR* is one *locus classicus* of this debate), but we were agreed about their significance. In my view, much that was creative, albeit chaotic and impressionistic, about the 'picture of the world' which came from the pages of New Left writing owed its freshness and vitality (as well as its utopianism) to the effort to sketch the meanings of these rapidly shifting contours of change. That is indeed one place where the New Left investment in the debate about *culture* first arose. First, because it was in the cultural and ideological domain that social change appeared to be making itself most dramatically visible. Second, because the cultural dimension seemed to us not a secondary, but a constitutive dimension of society. (This reflects part of the New Left's long-standing quarrel with the reductionism and economism of the base–superstructure metaphor.) Third, because the discourse of culture seemed to us fundamentally necessary to any language in which socialism could be redescribed. The

New Left therefore took the first faltering steps of putting questions of cultural analysis and cultural politics at the centre of its politics.

In these different ways, the New Left launched an assault on the narrow definition of 'politics' and tried to project in its place an 'expanded conception of the political'. If it did not move so far as the feminist principle that 'the personal is political', it certainly opened itself up to the critical dialectic between 'private troubles' and 'public issues', which blew the conventional conception of politics apart. The logic implied by our position was that these 'hidden dimensions' had to be represented within the discourses of 'the political' and that ordinary people could and should organize where they were, around issues of immediate experience; begin to articulate their dissatisfactions in an existential language and build an agitation from that point. (This was the source of our much-debated 'socialist humanism'.) The expanded defin- ition of the political also entailed a recognition of the proliferation of the potential sites of social conflict and the constituencies for change. Although we were in favour of a strong trade unionism, we contested the idea that *only* those at the 'point of production' could make the revolution.

In our report in *NLR* 1 on the London Club's work in Notting Hill, for example, we spoke of racial oppression, housing, property deteri- oration and short-sighted urban planning alongside the more traditional themes of poverty and unemployment; we spoke of young Blacks on the street while youth clubs were closed, working mothers without crèches and children without playgrounds, as equally central to any modern conception of the 'degradations' of modern capitalism – though we remained blind to the ways in which even this expanded conception of politics was still inscribed in gendered categories. Doubtless this over- expanded definition traced the connections between different domains very weakly and blurred the cutting edge of our strategy, but it was the inevitable outcome of a powerful belief that the language of socialism *must* address the question of 'how we live now and how we ought to live'.

The critique of reformism and its singularly British representative, 'Labourism', was entailed in this enlarged discourse of 'the political'. In the light of Stalinism and the Cold War, reformism appeared the obvious, rational alternative for anyone who wished to redistribute wealth more evenly and have a more socially just society, but who was also committed to the 'civilized values' of the Western world. Edward Thompson described this Hobson's choice, in his article in *Out of Apathy*, as an Orwellian dilemma. We looked for a more radical and structural transformation of society: partly because we were committed to many of the fundamental perspectives of the classical socialist

programme; partly because we saw in modern capitalism a greater, not a
lesser, concentration of social power and could trace the impact of
'commodification' in areas of life far removed from the immediate sites
of wage-labour exploitation – but above all because of the much broader
critique we had of 'capitalist civilization and culture'. Questions of alienation, the breakdown of community, the weakness of democracy in civil
society and what the early American New Left, in its Port Huron statement, called 'quality of life' issues, constituted for us as significant an
indictment of the present regime of capital as any other – an indictment
we thought irremediable within an unreformed and untransformed
society and culture. No one expressed the fundamental and constitutive
character of this argument for and within the New Left more profoundly
than Raymond Williams.

It was in this sense that we remained 'revolutionaries', though few
retained any faith in a vanguardist seizure of state power by a small
minority unaccompanied by any broader democratic and cultural 'long
revolution', or a shift in the 'mode of production' achieved by bureaucratic state control. Both seemed implausible scenarios under conditions
of modern class democracies, and unlikely to produce those automatic
transformations which the traditional left anticipated. The opposition
between 'reform' and 'revolution' seemed to many of us outdated: more
a way of swearing at and anathematizing others than having any real
analytic–historical value in its own right. We sought, in different ways, to
bypass it.

In these and other significant ways, the dominant tendency of the
New Left was 'revisionist' (then not such a dirty word as now) with
respect both to Labourism and to Marxism. We had come into existence
and now lived in the age of 'many Marxisms'. We confronted the 'freez-
ing' of Marxism in Eastern Europe into a sterile state dogma. We
watched 'Marxist' tanks overthrowing the 'Marxist' provisional government of Imre Nagy and Georg Lukács in Hungary. The 'Reasoners'
occupied this revisionist space in one way – as Communist dissidents.
The 'ULR-ers' occupied it in another way, for most of our generation
had entered politics *through* the debate with orthodox and doctrinal
versions of Marxism. Few, if any, of us could have been described, after
1956, as 'orthodox' – principally because, though we held different
positions about how much of Marxism could be transposed without
'revision' to the second half of the twentieth century, all of us refused to
regard it as a fixed and finished doctrine or sacred text. For example, of
considerable importance to some of us was the rediscovery, through
Chuck Taylor, of Marx's early *Economic and Philosophical Manuscripts*, with its themes of alienation, species being and 'new needs',
which he brought over from Paris in 1958 in French and which only

shortly thereafter became available to us in an English translation.

There were many other 'themes' which any comprehensive account would be obliged to discuss: for example, the debate around 'socialist humanism', the analyses of the Third World and, in connection with CND, 'neutralism', NATO and disarmament; the debates about popular culture and the media. However, since the New Left is so often 'tagged' as mainly an intellectual formation, it may be more appropriate to remind readers that the 'first' New Left, however mistakenly, thought of itself as a 'movement' rather than simply a 'journal', and that only with the passage to the 'second' generation in the early 1960s was this project abandoned.

Shortly after the publication of the first issue, *ULR* called its first 'readers' meeting' on an inauspicious Sunday afternoon, which was followed by the foundation of the London *ULR* Club. For its first meetings, the four editors invited the distinguished contributors to the first issue to address their readers. The first speaker was Isaac Deutscher, whose title, 'The Red Sixties', proved not quite as prophetic as it sounds, since Deutscher predicted, not '1968', but the dramatic changes in the Soviet Union which he was convinced would quickly follow the Khrushchev revelations. This was a huge, exciting occasion, and large beyond all expectations. The four editors rearranged the room in the Royal Hotel in what Raphael Samuel assured us was the intimate manner of the Berlin political cafés of the thirties and went off to have a meal. When we returned, there were seven hundred people waiting outside the building, and one or two (including Suzy Benghiat, later to be a leading figure in the London New Left Club), had drafted themselves to set an entrance price and take the money.

In the early years the *ULR* Club (later the London New Left Club) attracted to its weekly meetings audiences of three and four hundred drawn from across the whole spectrum of the left. For a time it provided an extremely important, lively, often contentious focal point for people with no other formal political commitment. It differed from the typical 'left' organization or sect in that its purpose was *not* to recruit members but to engage with the political culture of the left on a very broad front through argument, debate, discussion and education. It became an important independent centre for left politics in London, particularly after it found a permanent home, through another of Raphael Samuel's nerve-rackingly risky but brilliantly innovative ventures, in the Partisan coffee bar in Carlisle Street. This was the first left 'coffee bar' in London, with a club house and library on the floors above, which had been lovingly redesigned by Ernest Rodker, a fine carpenter and one of the most active and committed club members. On the fourth floor it housed the offices of *ULR* with its one full-time employee: Janet Hase, the Australian business manager. After the merger, they became the offices of *NLR*. However, weekly club meetings continued to take place in larger venues around central London, since the Partisan was too small to house them. Following the merger, a number of 'New Left clubs' sprang up around the country. (The last issue of *NLR* which I edited, no. 12, listed thirty-nine in various stages of political health.)

A brief description of the activities of the London Left Club will give some indication of what this 'movement' around New Left ideas was like. There were well-publicized and large weekly public meetings with a very wide range of speakers. Gaitskell, Crosland, Crossman and others from the Labour leadership came to debate with us. A range of smaller discussion groups flourished around the Club, including an Education, a Literature, a Teachers' and a Schools group. The cultural debates and activities were considered as important as the more 'political' ones. Arnold Wesker and John Arden connected us to the 'new drama' and its home at the Royal Court; Lindsay Anderson, Karel Reisz and Alex Jacobs to Free Cinema, the British Film Institute and the National Film Theatre; Paddy Whannel and others to the London jazz scene; Roger Mayne to new movements in documentary photography; Germano Facetti and Robin Fior to new ideas in design and typography. There were visits to and discussions at new venues like the Whitechapel Gallery.

The position of the Club in central London, the fact that many of us were secondary-modern teachers – coupled with pressures from 'friends' of the Club, like Colin MacInnes, about the failure of the left to put down roots in this emerging post-war culture or to recruit 'modern' young people to its cause – gave the New Left Club an uncertain 'stake' in the emerging youth culture of the period. (Under the influence of MacInnes, I wrote about this aspect of the New Left in 'Absolute Beginnings' in the final issue of *ULR*.) Inevitably the London Club became part of the wider metropolitan culture and the Partisan was, for a time, a key point in the subterranean culture of Soho life. Other clubs reflected, in programme and composition, the cultural and political character of their localities: the Manchester and Hull Left Clubs were close to the local labour movement; the Fife Socialist League was linked, through Lawrence Daly, to an independent socialist movement amongst Fife miners in Scotland, the Croydon and Hemel Hempstead Clubs had a more 'cross-class' or even '*déclassé*-new-town' feel to them.

Very early on, the London New Left Club pioneered in central London the propaganda and leafleting for the first CND Aldermaston March, which the club membership supported *en masse*. This was the beginning of close links between the New Left, the modern peace movement in Britain and the birth of CND as a mass political organization.

The clubs also mounted a sustained propaganda campaign in relation to the policy debates in the Labour Party about the 'revision of Clause 4'. Gaitskell himself had inserted the cultural question into this political agenda when he argued after the 1959 defeat that Labour's social base had been permanently eroded by 'the telly, the fridge and the second-hand motorcar'. Pessimists might like to know that we spoke quite openly at the time of 'Fifteen years of Tory rule? Mr Selwyn Lloyd's finger on the trigger? Mr Lennox Boyd's rifles over Africa? Mr Macmillan's face on TV? *Again?*'. The Club engaged with the full range of these themes. We published replies to Labour Party discussion documents, debated the Crosland theses on which they were based, set up exhibitions on cultural issues at Labour Party conferences. We mounted, for example, the first – and only? – exhibition at an annual Labour Party Conference offering a political critique of commercial advertising. We also produced a free, cyclostyled daily broadsheet for delegates, *This Week*. I am proud to say that it was in its pages that I first described Harold Wilson as 'Mr Facing-Both-Ways'.

Among its other activities, the New Left Club in London became deeply involved in 1958 with the race riots in Notting Hill and with the anti-racist struggles of the period around North Kensington. We participated in the efforts to establish tenants' associations in the area, helped to protect black people who, at the height of the 'troubles', were molested and harassed by white crowds in an ugly mood between Notting Hill station and their homes, and picketed the Mosley and National Front meetings. George Clark, who later pioneered an early form of 'community politics' in North Kensington, first cut his teeth on this experience. Michael DeFreitas – later to have another career as 'Malcolm X' – was one of the 'street hustlers' who, as a result of this intervention, came over to the side of the tenants he had been hired to hassle. In the course of this work we first stumbled across the powerful traces of racism inside the local Labour Party itself, and Rachel Powell, an active club member, unearthed the scandal of 'Rachmanism' and white landlord exploitation in Notting Hill, but failed to persuade the media to take it seriously until it later surfaced as a side-show to the Profumo Affair.

Peter Sedgwick once acutely observed that the New Left was less a movement than a 'milieu'. He was noting the lack of tight organizational structure, the loose conception of leadership, the flat hierarchies, the absence of membership, rules, regulations, party programme or 'line' which characterized the New Left, in sharp contrast with other political tendencies and sects on the far left. These organizational features were the product of our critique of Leninist and democratic centralist forms of organization and the emphasis on self-organization and participatory politics, which we can now see retrospectively as 'prefigurative' of so much that was to come afterwards. He may also have been obliquely commenting on the low level of working-class participation – or, to be more accurate, the 'cross-class competition' of many, though by no means all, of the New Left clubs. This could be seen as – and indeed was – a serious weakness, but oddly enough, it also had some compensations. Where the clubs were particularly strong was in those social strata emerging within and across the rapidly shifting, recomposing-decomposing class landscapes of post-war Britain. This separated us, not from ordinary working people, for we had many of those as active supporters, but from the political cultures of the traditional labour movement and the revolutionary cadres of the sects. Nevertheless, it gave the New Left a privileged access to the grinding, grating processes of contradictory social change.

With all their weaknesses, the clubs signified the project of the New Left to be a new kind of socialist entity: not a party but a 'movement of ideas'. We aimed to constitute an intervention in British political life and to develop a self-organizing and participatory political practice which would be prefigurative of socialism itself – and an effective critique of the political practices typical of either the major parties or the left sects. It was said that by 1962–63 many Left clubs were in decline – and so they were. But that is not the point. The clubs and other 'movement' aspects of the 'first' New Left were not only symptomatic of our politics but a sign that, for us and for the left, the *'question of agency'* had become deeply problematic. The 'second' New Left – which began, after a brief, brilliant interlude of 'troika' rule, with Perry Anderson's accession to the editorship, the restructuring of the editorial board and the exodus of many of the 'old' New Left members – was a much more rigorous theoretical project committed to a more orthodox, less 'revisionist', reading of Marxism, and was pursued with remarkable flair and single-mindedness. But it was *not* a project which constituted the question of political agency as in any way problematic, either theoretically or strategically.

These questions of political organization, strategy and style are best exemplified in relation to certain concrete political questions of the time, though they may be thought to have wider implications. CND and the Labour Party are perhaps the most useful examples. Peggy Duff, General Secretary of CND and the outstanding organizer of the anti-nuclear movement in that period, subsequently wrote, in her book *Left, Left, Left*, that in the end, CND swallowed up the New Left. I do not agree with this judgement, but I understand what lay behind it. Once involved, the New Left gave CND its sustained and unqualified support. Their fates became closely intertwined and indeed, both experienced a related decline in the mid 1960s. Nevertheless, the New Left also had a project in relation to CND: to broaden its politics; to 'educate', in Gramsci's sense, the moral impulses which brought most people to the peace movement into a wider politics of the left; and to make explicit the connections between 'the bomb', capitalism, NATO, Stalinism, the Warsaw Pact. But we pursued that project through an 'open' rather than a sectarian strategy. We were committed to working alongside CND, rather than operating parasitically on it.

This was in sharp contrast to the 'hard' left and Trotskyist sects, who by and large adopted a cynical but classically sectarian practice towards CND. They treated the peace movement as a 'soft' recruiting ground: to them, it was a movement dominated by misguided moral and religious enthusiasts, a few of whom could, however, be picked off for a more 'serious' enterprise and parachuted into the nitty-gritty of 'real politics' somewhere else. In this conception, 'real politics' is so often not where everybody else is, but always 'somewhere else'. The Trotskyists were to do exactly the same thing again with young people and students in 1968, picking off recruits from the student movement for a few heady months of selling 'the paper' outside the factory gates before, brutalized by this entirely gestural mimicry of revolutionary politics, the young recruits made good their escape, once and for all, from left politics of any kind.

We adopted this approach partly out of conviction, partly because we thought the movement of ordinary people *into* politics – breaking with the crust of conventional opinions and orthodox alignments in their own lives, on a concrete issue, and beginning to 'take action for themselves' – was more politically significant than the most correct of 'correct lines'. Those foxed by such references to 'correctness' may like to recall that one had to debate as a serious issue the question of whether or not the Soviet bomb was a 'Workers' Bomb' and therefore more worth keeping than the capitalist one. Another reason was that we saw in embryo in CND a new kind of political mobilization – beyond, so to speak, the big party battalions – which reflected certain emergent social forces and aspirations characteristic of their time, in relation to which it was necessary for the left to develop a new political practice.

CND was one of the first of this type of 'social movement' to appear in post-war politics – a popular movement with a clear radical thrust and an implicit 'anti-capitalist' content, formed through self-activity in civil society around a concrete issue, but lacking a clear class composition and appealing to people across the clear-cut lines of traditional class identity or organizational loyalties. It was already possible to recognize, in these new movements, features of modern society, and points of social antagonism which – like the civil-rights movement at the time, and feminist and sexual questions, ecological and environmental issues, community politics, welfare rights and anti-racist struggles in the 1970s and 1980s – have proved difficult to construct within the organizational agendas of the traditional left. Without these social movements, however, no contemporary mass political mobilization or movement for radical change in modern times is now conceivable.

Moreover, the New Left itself belonged to the same conjuncture as CND. It was the product of the same decay in the 'relations of representation' between the people, the classes and the parties which has become so much more pronounced in the 1970s and 1980s and mobilized similar social forces. As we wrote in the last issue of *ULR*:

> Here is a movement of people drawn from very different backgrounds, tired of the two-way shuffle of the political party bureaucracies, fed up with the Cold War slogans of 'massive retaliation' and the 'Two Camps' cast of mind, terrified by what C. Wright Mills calls 'the drift and thrust' to World War III. We cannot claim credit for the vigour and success of this movement, but we have been proud to contribute to it, and, through the journals and the clubs, to develop some of its socialist implications. Similarly with the movements of protest against the Hola Camp atrocities and the Nyasaland 'crisis'. Such groups of people find a common cause with us, not merely because of the individual issues but because, by doing so, they are helping to establish the only basis upon which socialism can be built: the principle that, whatever kind of world we want, we are going to have to make it for ourselves and the sooner we stand up, say what it is, and fight for it, the quicker it will be in coming. If the *New Left Review* has any political roots, they will be *there*. Without CND supporters, Anti-Ugly protesters [a protest movement against the banality and conformism of post-war British architecture], African demonstrators, Free Cinema and the Society for the Abolition of The Death Penalty, we would be nowhere.

Ultimately, what CND posed for the New Left – as the new social movements always do – was the problem of how to articulate these new impulses and social forces with the more traditional class politics of the left; and how, through this articulation, the project of the left could be transformed. The fact that we had no greater success than the left has had since in trying to construct a 'historical bloc' out of such heterogeneous social interests, political movements and agendas, in building a hegemonic political practice out of, and with, these differences, does not negate the urgency of the task. What we can 'learn' from the 'first' New Left here is what questions to ask, not which answers work. (Two decades later feminism found itself log-jammed in the same place, caught between the 'Vanguards' and the 'Fragments'.) On the other hand, the failure to resolve it had – and has – consequences. There is no question that the 'first' New Left was weakened by its failure to find a

strategic way through this dilemma and remained somewhat disaggre-
gated between its very different constituencies.

As far as the Labour Party was concerned, many people in and
around the New Left were members of the Labour Party. Many were
not. As a movement, our attitude to the Labour Party was quite clear.
Our independence from organizational links, controls, party routines
and discipline was essential for our political project. The majority vote
for unilateralism at the Labour Party Conference, for which many of us
campaigned, was a clear example to us of 'defeat-in-victory', as a result
of mistaking a platform victory for the winning of new popular political
positions. Inside the machine, CND withered and shrivelled into a talis-
man, a fetish of party conference resolutions, plaything of the
manoeuvres of the block vote, without touching ground in the political
consciousness or activity of many actual people. It is still being defended
by the left in this fetishized form.

At the same time we recognized that the fate of socialism in Britain
was inextricably bound up with the fate and fortunes of Labour. We
recognized Labour as, for good or ill, the Party which had hegemonized
the vast majority of the organized working class with a reformist politics.
We honoured its historic links to the trade-union movement. We
acknowledged it as the engine of the 'welfare state' revolution of 1945,
which we never underestimated because it represented a reform, rather
than an overthrow, of the system. We remained deeply critical of the
Fabian and Labourist cultures of the Labour Party, of its 'statism', its
lack of popular roots in the political and cultural life of ordinary people,
its bureaucratic suspicion of any independent action or 'movement'
outside its limits, and its profound anti-intellectualism. We opposed the
deeply undemocratic procedures of the block vote and the Party's empty
'constitutionalism'. Yet we knew that the Labour Party represented,
whether we liked it or not, the strategic *stake* in British politics, which no
one could ignore.

We therefore developed an open and polemical politics in relation to
the Gaitskell leadership, on the one hand, and the 'nothing-has-
changed, reaffirm-Clause-4' perspective of the traditional left on the
other; taking up – here as elsewhere – a third position, opening a 'third
front'. In the revisionist debates of the 1950s and 1960s we opposed the
post-capitalist, 'human face of corporate capitalism' theses proposed in
Crosland's *The Future of Socialism* while recognizing him as a formidable and intelligent opponent. In relation to the left, we insisted –
against the doctrinal immobilism of much of the Labour and trade-union
left – on the necessity of grounding the perspectives of the left in a new
analysis of the novel conditions of post-war capitalism and social
change. Some people would continue to work for this inside the Labour

Party; others worked outside. We did not see how there could be a 'correct' line on this issue when there was so little relationship between what people wanted politically and the vehicle for achieving it. Our strategy was therefore to sidestep it and instead to involve people, whatever their affiliations, in independent political activity and debate. As we wrote in *ULR* 6, 'for the first time since the war, there is, particularly among young people, a left movement which is not the prisoner of any sect, and yet which is not to be automatically won to the Labour Party, even as an opposition within it.'

This 'parallel' strategy required, as its necessary condition, the maintenance of journals and clubs, a network of contacts, forms of demonstration, argument and propaganda which articulated this 'third position', which were not subject to the routines of Transport House but were nevertheless designed to break back into and have an effect on the internal politics of the Labour Party and the labour movement. We called this strategy (subsequently treated with scathing irony by some *enragés* of the New Left Mark 2 during the High Noon of 1968, but in hindsight not so simple or foolish a 'war of position' as they made it appear) the strategy of 'one foot in, one foot out'.

What type of organizational leadership did these strategies presuppose? The metaphor to which we constantly returned was that of 'the socialist propaganda'. As Edward Thompson put it in the final issue of *The New Reasoner*:

> The New Left does not propose itself as an alternative organization to those already in the field; rather, it offers two things to those within and without the existing organizations – a specific propaganda of ideas, and certain practical services (journals, clubs, schools, etc).

The notion of a 'socialist propaganda of ideas' was, of course, borrowed directly and explicitly from William Morris and the relationships forged in the Socialist League between intellectuals, struggling to make themselves what Gramsci called 'organic', and the working class. We had all read and been inspired by the 'Making Socialists' chapter of Edward Thompson's *William Morris: Romantic to Revolutionary*. Indeed, the first editorial of *NLR* was framed at either end by a quote from Morris's *Commonweal* article of July 1885: 'The Labour Movement is not in its insurrectionary phase.' I added: 'we are in our missionary phase.'

Although it was not, as they say these days, 'fully theorized', this conception of leadership was based on certain clear presuppositions. The first was the necessity of challenging the conventional anti-intellectualism of the British labour movement and overcoming the traditional division between intellectuals and the working class. The second was the repudiation of three alternative models: 'vanguardist' and 'democratic centralist' conceptions of revolutionary leadership; Fabian notions of the middle-class 'experts' giving socialism from within the state machine to the working classes; and the traditional Labour left faith in constitutional mechanisms, conference resolutions, winning the block votes and 'electoral contests with slightly more "left" candidates'. Third, our view was that changes in British society had brought a large number of the new, post-war social strata within reach of socialist education and propaganda. Fourth, we had a deep conviction that against the 'economism' of the Stalinist, Trotskyist and Labourist left alike, socialism was a *conscious* democratic movement and socialists were *made*, not born or 'given' by the inevitable laws of history or the objective processes of the mode of production alone.

We also challenged the prevailing view that social change as such, even the so-called 'affluent society', would objectively and of itself erode the appeal of socialist propaganda and that socialism could arise only out of immiseration and degradation. Our emphasis on people taking action for themselves, 'building socialism from below' and 'in the here and now', not waiting for some abstract Revolution to transform everything in the twinkling of an eye, proved, in the light of the re-emergence of these themes after 1968, strikingly prefigurative (despite all the other differences between the New Lefts of '1956' and '1968').

As we put it in *NLR* 1:

> We have to go into towns and cities, universities and technical colleges, youth clubs and Trade Union branches and – as Morris said – *make socialists* there. We have come through 200 years of capitalism and 100 years of imperialism. Why should people – naturally – turn to socialism? There is no law which says that the Labour Movement, like a great inhuman engine, is going to throb its way into socialism or that we can, any longer . . . rely upon poverty and exploitation to drive people, like blind animals, towards socialism. Socialism is, and will remain, an active faith in a new society, to which we turn as conscious, thinking human beings. People have to be confronted with experience, called to the 'society of equals', not because they have never had it so bad, but because the 'society of equals' is better than the best soft-selling consumer capitalist society, and life is something *lived*, not something one passes through like tea through a strainer.

This position may seem naive and has certainly been dubbed 'utopian' and 'populist' since. But it was populist in the 'Narodnik' sense of 'going to the people' and in terms of what they/we might become, rather than in the Thatcherite sense of massaging popular consent by cynical appeals to what the people are said by their betters to want. We had an instinctive, if not well formulated, notion that the socialist project had to be rooted in the 'here and now' and connect with lived experience: with what we have since learned to call 'the national-popular'. 'The people' is, of course, always a discursive construction and the blurring of a precise social referent in the populism of the early New Left was certainly significant. But there is more than one kind of 'populism' and it can, despite all its problems, be articulated either to the right or the left, and serve either to short-circuit or to develop popular antagonisms. The 'populism' of the early New Left was certainly of the latter sort, as Edward Thompson, its main architect, put it in *The New Reasoner*:

> What will distinguish the New Left will be its rupture with the tradition of inner party factionalism, and its renewal of the tradition of open association, socialist education, and activity, directed towards the people as a whole. . . . It will insist that the Labour Movement is not a thing but an association of men and women; that working people are not the passive recipients of economic and cultural conditioning, but are intellectual and moral beings . . . it will appeal to people by rational argument and moral challenge. It will counter the philistine materialism and anti-intellectualism of the Old Left by appealing to the totality of human interests and potentialities, and by constructing new channels of communication between industrial workers and experts in the sciences and arts. It will cease to postpone the satisfactions of Socialism to an hypothetic period 'after the Revolution', but will seek to promote in the present and in particular in great centres of working class life, a richer sense of community.

Needless to say, the tensions and contradictions implicit in this 'populism' were never wholly resolved. The rapid shifts in social structure of the post-war period, which we constantly tried to characterize without pinning them down precisely, cut unevenly into the New Left and we failed to build these differences into a new 'historical bloc', though that was our implicit aim. The tensions already alluded to between the provincial 'North' and cosmopolitan 'London', like later versions of the 'North/South' divide, were much more complex than this simple opposition suggests. Nevertheless, they shadowed some critical differences in the pace and character of class recomposition and social decomposition in post-war British society and came to stand metonymically for the diversifying ground of politics, without providing any principle of articulation. The tensions between 'intellectuals' and 'activists' were a continuing, if largely unspoken, problem connected to the much wider issue of the uncertain status of intellectuals in English cultural life generally and the disabling philistinism of the left. Cutting across all these tensions from another direction was the almost totally hidden question of gender – the fact that the great majority of the editorial-board leadership were men and that many of those on whom the actual 'labour' of keeping the whole enterprise going fell were women: the usual sexual division of labour, reproduced so often in the left. About this last question the New Left preserved – as did the rest of the left – a profound unconsciousness.

We hoped that the clubs would develop their own independent organization, leadership and channels of communication (perhaps their own newsheet or bulletin), leaving the journal free to develop its own project. But we lacked the resources to bring this about, which exacerbated in the clubs feelings that they had no control over the journal, and in the editorial board the fear that a journal of ideas could not be effectively run by committees. It was, in effect, this last issue and the cross-pressures associated with it which finally precipitated my own resignation from the editorship of *New Left Review* in 1961.

It is not for me to attempt any overall assessment of the 'first' New Left, which I see as only a first stage in the constitution of a new kind of left politics. It seems absurd to attempt to defend its record in detail or to impose, retrospectively, a consistency it did not possess. Its strengths and weaknesses, errors and mistakes, remain and are unanswerable – to be learned from rather than repudiated. Nevertheless I would make the sharpest distinction between what we did and how we did it, and the wider project. I remain as committed to the latter, thirty years later, as I was then. The 'third space' which the 'first' New Left defined and tried to prise open still seems to me the only hope for the renewal of the democratic and socialist project in our new and bewildering times.

2

Born-again Socialism*

Raphael Samuel

Members of the early New Left aspired to be innovative and original, breaking with the orthodoxies of traditional socialism and align-
ing themselves with the protest of the 'angry young men' of the
post-war generation. Raphael Samuel argues that despite their
'modern' rhetoric they continued to interpret capitalist society in the
traditional terms of class struggle, and in their projects shared the
reformist impulse of the post-war Labour government. Rather than
constituting the beginning of a 'new' socialism, Samuel concludes,
the early new Left marked the end of old-style socialist politics.

*This is part of a three-part essay on the New Left to be published by Verso in
1989 in *Theatres of Memory*. Footnotes have been omitted from the present
version.

Members of the New Left, as the name suggests, were modernizers. In our own self-perception we were forward-looking and iconoclastic, breaking with age-old shibboleths, 'picking up the quick tissues in the society, sloughing off the dead'. We prided ourselves on addressing 'contemporary' reality, and in particular the new forms of consumerism which were remaking capitalism and class. In industry we looked to the future rather than the past, being more concerned with the effects of automation on the labour process than with strikes. In education we took up arms against an 'obsolete' system 'contradicting . . . the main trends in contemporary British society'. We championed more child-orientated pedagogies and attacked the socially divisive. The public schools were 'forces of inertia', bastions of resistance to 'radical social change'. The 'collar-and-tie smartness' of the grammar-school uniform was 'absurd', the grammar-school ethos a 'training in caste assumptions', and its mode of government authoritarian. (An early article in *ULR* looks forward to the replacement of the prefectorial system 'by some type of school democracy'.) The eleven-plus, which condemned the majority of British schoolchildren to the secondary modern schools, was not only an outrage: it was also, from the point of view of technical education and economic development, 'a tragic waste'.

In housing and town planning we stood for comprehensive redevelopment, advocating 'islands of compact buildings' or 'towns within cities' as an alternative to 'subtopia' and sprawl. Vallingby, Stockholm, was one of our models, 'the new attractive LCC flats at Roehampton' another – high-rise blocks on a site 'formerly . . . wasted by crumbling, decaying and totally uneconomic Victorian mansions'. In the same spirit we championed the new building techniques and 'open-plan' layouts pioneered by Hertfordshire County Council in its primary schools. We also presented ourselves – improbable as it may seem in the light of later revulsion – as avatars of the motorcar age, praising, in *ULR* 2, the 'great sculptural beauty' of the new Los Angeles flyovers and attacking the British road system as 'archaic'. Here too, as in housing, piecemeal 'tinkering' was counterposed to comprehensive development. Our architects gave enthusiastic endorsement to that licence for the destruction of the traditional shopping street, the Buchanan Report; while Stuart Hall, in the first *Out of Apathy*, complained of the motorway programme (the scheme for English *Autobahnen* which at that stage had stalled at the building of the M1) being no more than a pathetic 'squiggle' on the map.

In art politics, the New Left – or at any rate the *ULR* end of it – was on the side of the avant-garde, one of the invisible differences with our elder brethren on *The New Reasoner* and in the outcome, after the two journals merged, an explosive one. Bred on – or attuned to – the modern movement, we published an excited, combative obituary of Wyndham Lewis in *ULR* 2 and were even, at this stage (correspondence of the time reveals), thinking of soliciting an article from Ezra Pound. We defended abstract art against its Establishment detractors, tilting a lance, in an early issue, against the President of the Royal Academy. Our showcase in London, 'Better Books', was determinedly contemporary, with art college students as shop assistants, Modernist panels and Braque motifs. It was to play some small part in the *Lady Chatterley* trial, defying the censor to put the Penguin edition on sale; and its poetry readings and 'happenings' were an early nursery of 1960s counterculture. Bauhaus was one of our unofficial enthusiasms, perhaps through the medium of the young architects who gathered about us in London; sans-serif typography (again much influenced by our London recruits) another. A feature of early *ULR* publications and notices is a preference for hard, bold lines.

Intellectually, too, we believed ourselves to be exploring new frontiers. We championed sociology as a new learning which would introduce the breath of life into the universities and make traditional subjects more 'relevant'. We were also, in our early days, sympathetic to the claims of science, believing, with others at the time, that the number of scientists and technologists in the universities should be increased, and the gap between science and the humanities closed. In philosophy we argued for a more phenomenological understanding of reality, contrasting the urgencies of Merleau-Ponty and Sartre with the frivolities of Oxford philosophy. One of the excitements of the New Left – or anyway, the *ULR* – was the discovery of new texts which allowed the socialist idea to be argued for in fresh terms. Wright Mills's '*magnum opus* on the American Power Elite' was one of the books which performed this function in our early days, a model for our work on *The Insiders*. A later discovery, which can be dated fairly precisely to the summer of 1957, was alienation theory and the young Marx. It gave us a 'humanist' Marx – the Marx of the *Economic and Philosophical Manuscripts* of 1844 – to counterpose to the 'determinist' Marx of later years. This early Marx was in some sense, so far as Britain was concerned, our very own, since the *Manuscripts* were not translated into English until 1960.

More pertinently, we found in 'alienation' a term which spoke to those who felt themselves 'outsiders' in British society. In terms of political advocacy it gave a new dignity and sweep to our argument, a unifying concept which reinforced our critique of capitalism with arguments from philosophy. In the New Left it rapidly came to occupy the imaginative space accorded to 'exploitation' in earlier schools of socialist thought, and 'hegemony' in more recent ones. Newcomers took to it as a kind of flagship. 'If there is one word which the Labour Party lacks,' wrote Perry Anderson – anticipating, as an undergraduate, one of the themes he was later to develop as editor of *New Left Review* – 'it is alienation.'

Within socialism, the New Left called for a 'conscious break' with the past. We did not, like our comrades in the 'old' left (the Bevanites and the 'ginger groups' in the Labour Party) call for a return to 'the spirit of the pioneers', but looked instead for ways in which socialism could be made anew, 'a living thing' freed of the orthodoxies which deformed it. Communism (or what we called Stalinism) was 'socialist theory which has lost the essential ingredient of humanity'. It was a 'socialism of the heavy industrial base' which sacrificed the people on the altar of economic growth and delivered them up to the rule of a Party autocracy. Social democracy was hardly better, a 'tarted-up'* version of welfare capitalism 'in which creative, popular and intellectual initiative was at a low ebb, bureaucracy – particularly in administration, trade unions and nationalized industries – at full flood'. The Labour Party was dominated by careerists, 'those parliamentary frumps* whose sense of principle has long been dowsed among three-line whips, block-vote intrigues, vote-catching expediencies'. 'Narrowly empirical' where communism was 'dogmatically theoretical', it lacked imagination, taking refuge in ancient verities while its constituencies melted away. It had surrendered the pass to the Conservatives on the arms race. It had accommodated itself to the Cold War. It was powerless to resist the onward march of consumerism.

As opposed to Labour orthodoxy, we called for a new kind of politics: one which drew strength from movements outside the framework

---

*Discussion of such misogynist terms is taken up in the extended essay.

of the traditional parties and took as its starting point the spirit of youth. The choice, as we defined it, was between Ancients and Moderns. The Labour Party, as at present constituted, was a monument to its past, 'an ageing body of veterans, shedding 75,000 supporters each year and carrying high slogans which are becoming increasingly irrelevant to those who were born since the thirties'. At the other end of the age spectrum there was CND, 'to an unprecedented degree a movement of young people', the Aldermaston marches, 'very much the political coming of age of a generation . . . overwhelmingly . . . the under twenty-fives, and the new forms of cultural politics. Unless the Labour Party could find ways of speaking to them, it would wither on the vine.

ULR, or at least that influential fraction of it which became increasingly preoccupied with 'youth culture' and the popular arts, prided itself on being street-wise. 'ULR-ers' dressed sharply and danced coolly. In the idiom of the day, they were 'hip' – a term, or fantasy self, coined by Norman Mailer, writing on 'The White Negroes' in *Dissent*, our sister publication in New York. Like Colin MacInnes in his metropolitan ramblings (some of which we published), they discovered in working-class adolescents the rebels and outsiders of our time. 'Hip' was a term which spread like wildfire, though it made some of us uncomfortable. Even so respectable a character as Paul Rose, an ambitious young lawyer who was then secretary of the Manchester Left Club, later a Labour MP and later still a defector to the SDP, found occasion to use it, though with a characteristically provincial twist. 'There is no place for socialist "squares" in the age of Humphrey Lyttelton, Aldermaston and Manchester United', he writes in *NLR*, advocating football, cinema, hiking, art and the Hallé Orchestra ('our world') as a putative Labour alternative to the Young Conservatives' barbecues and hunt balls.

The generational idiom was quite crucial to the New Left's sense of its own modernity. It made the age gap as significant a lever of change as the older class divisions. It encouraged us to conceptualize political issues in terms of 'Ancients and Moderns' and to treat our adversaries as by definition 'old-fashioned' and 'out of date'. 'Dream boys', the working-class male adolescents on whom both the *ULR* and *NLR* turned a fascinated gaze, to some extent took the place of the absent – or sleeping – proletariat as a force for protest. Their emergent lifestyles were lovingly chronicled; their gestures were interpreted in terms of refusal; and they were credited with rebellious desires remarkably akin to those of the writers who spoke in their name:

> Instinctively, young working-class people are radical. They hate the stuffiness of the class system, though they cannot give it a political name; they hate the frustrations of petty conservative officialdom, though they cannot spell

'bureaucracy'. But they feel and encounter these things in private, emotional ways, for this is how adolescence encounters the world. . . . Politically, they have no categories by means of which to distinguish between the corrupt conservative Trade Union official they meet at the works, and the shiny, corrupt boss who is probably a prospective Tory MP. These two often *look* to them as if they're on the same side. They *sound* as if they're saying the same thing. Perhaps they are . . .

The *ULR* had presented itself from the first as a movement of young people and offered itself as a forum where 'the generation of the thirties' and the 'generation of the fifties' could meet. The point of address was originally to socialists, but with the success of the *Review* it broadened out to a wider constituency. We knew – or believed we knew, because they were in our inner circle – that we spoke for what an editorial calls 'the scholarship boy generation', and we also came to believe that we were a political voice for the tens of thousands of young people who had materialized out of nowhere to give the Aldermaston marches their mass following. In another register, *ULR*, by its increasing involvement with the secondary modern schools and youth clubs, was credited with having a hot line to the alienated and the disaffected; by 1958 they were a major subject matter of the *Review*.

In sum, we came to think that there was an elective affinity between protest politics and generational revolt. *The New Reasoner*, though edited by what seemed to us a much older age group – war veterans, even if some of them were still in their thirties – also began, if more hesitantly, to adopt a generational idiom; and in its valedictory editorial, as the merger of the two journals approached, pictured the emergent New Left as Labour's ambassadors to youth: 'the bureaucracy will hold the machine . . . the New Left will hold the passes between it and the younger generation.'

In retrospect, the rupture with the 'old' left looks much less decisive than it did to us at the time. The writers of the New Left had been formed in a prior socialism and in their very different and individual ways they were anxious to prove their loyalty to it, recycling old ideas under new terminologies and drawing up battle lines on terms inherited from the past. Analogy had a powerful influence on the New Left imagination, and we were by no means immune to that nostalgia of protest to which Jimmy Porter had given such eloquent expression in *Look Back in Anger*. Thus de Gaulle's seizure of power in 1958, backed by the colonels in Algeria, seemed to us at first an action replay of the Spanish Civil War on which we were, at that very moment, mounting an exhibition at Carlisle Street: our immediate response was the formation of an emergency committee to give hospitality to the expected influx of political refugees. Domestically, we were only too ready to see Conservatism as the lineal descendant of feudalism, colonialism and 'Old Corruption'. Home Counties or stockbroker-belt Conservatives were to us, in Stuart Hall's excellent phrase, 'the White settlers of the Surrey hills'; the merchant bankers, plotting their *coups* on the grouse moors, were landed aristocrats *redivivi*.

A particularly potent analogy was that between the military establishments of the day – preparing, we believed, a nuclear holocaust – and those who had been responsible in 1916 for the first day on the Somme – the battle in which 250,000 British soldiers had been sent to their death. Playing First World War analogies against those of the Second World War, which the Conservatives – attacking detente of any kind as 'appeasement' – were rather successfully, if bizarrely, appropriating to themselves, was a normal feature of CND argument, illustrating the perils of the arms race and the fatality of a Europe divided into two hostile camps. For those who had been brought up on the war poets – anyone, that is, who had taken sixth-form English at school – the analogy was a fearful one, and it was powerfully revivified in the 1950s by a literature of historic exposure; by the American anti-war film *Paths of Glory*; and most influentially in Joan Littlewood's *Oh, What a Lovely War* – a brilliant theatrical transposition of the message of CND. For some of us at least, marching to Aldermaston, sitting down in front of the War Office or being arrested in Trafalgar Square was a long-delayed settling of accounts for Passchendaele.

Whatever the New Left's innovations and ruptures, they left the basic categories of socialist thought – and the basic elements of the socialist imagination – untouched. In political economy, our new terminologies (borrowed, largely, from the United States) camouflaged a quite traditional socialist outlook which, as C.A.R. Crosland was to argue against us, 'was simply pre- or anti-revolutionist'. Capitalism – 'the system' – was still the main enemy, though we conceptualized it in terms of 'oligopoly' and our main line of attack was moral rather than economic. In our analysis of power at the top – for example, in *The Insiders*, *The Controllers* and *'Bastard' Capitalism* – we expended a vast amount of energy attempting to prove that 'the managerial revolution' had not happened and that ownership and control were vested in the big corporations with the titled rich at their head. In *Out of Apathy* we depicted capitalism as a moribund social order whose race was nearly run – 'last-stage capitalism', as we hopefully designated it ('late capitalism' was the preferred term of the 1970s theoreticists) – a system, in E.P. Thompson's words, 'ripe' and 'overripe' for destruction. In a kindred vein we took up arms against Britain's *ancien régime*, its grouse-shooting merchant bankers, its caste-like institutions, its privileged schools. The New Left was convinced that the old ruling class was intact, and indeed a great deal of our empirical research – or 'power elite analysis – was devoted to mapping its contours. Our phraseology was determinedly up to date and sociological: the images which lay behind it were archaic.

Like other socialists, we focused a great deal of our attention on class divisions. Although we believed that 'simplified' versions of the class struggle had been 'discredited', we were no less insistent on the class nature of British society. The primacy of the working class was in our eyes unquestioned and we did not cease to speak of it as though it were a unified totality, though fastening on 'ways of life' rather than ways of struggle. We also subscribed to our own version of the 'labour metaphysic', anticipating one of Raymond Williams's major themes, when we argued in *ULR* 1 that the 'dominant feature' of society was 'the growing power' of the working class 'and, accompanying this, the gradual dispersion of political and economic control throughout the community'. Here is how Raymond Williams put it in *ULR* 2, treating 'party' and 'class' as a unity but transposing the key element in the couple from interests to values, and from industry to culture, community and the home:

> Working-class life is not primarily political, although it may often be seen as such from the outside or by abstraction. The political effect of working-class life is the product of the primary affections and allegiances in family and neighbourhood which . . . Richard Hoggart has so intelligently and eloquently described. Hoggart is wrong, however, in supposing that these are to be set on one side of a line, while on the other is set the wider social product – the Labour Movement – which he describes as the work of a minority. . . . A minority is normally thought of as isolated, self-defensive, opposed to the majority's values. The political and industrial leadership of the working class is, quite evidently, a minority of a different kind. It is not isolated, but is the articulate representation of an extension of primary values into the social fields. It is not self-defensive, for it seeks consistently to operate in the majority's behalf and interest. It is not opposed to majority values, but seeks to define them in wider terms. . . . Working-class materialism – the collective improvement of the common life – is, objectively, in our circumstances, a humane ideal. The primary affections run all the way through, for the working class sees no reason, in experience . . . why these primary values should not be made the values of society as a whole.

Our socialism was, in the last analysis, unproblematic. As an adjective, we used it as a floating signifier for anything we considered good, rather as Communists in the 1930s and 1940s had used the term 'progressive'. As a noun, it defined an ideal state of social being. As an idea, it represented the principle of hope. Whatever the crimes committed in its name, or the bureaucratic deformations to which it had been subject, its authority as a moral idea was unquestioned. It needed only to be cleansed of its Stalinist (or Fabian) encrustations for its original promise to be revealed. Politically modest, we were culturally imperialist in the claims which we made for it, insisting, against the 'piecemeal social engineering' favoured by reformists, that socialism involved a qualitative leap – or, in one of *ULR*'s favourite coinages, a 'breakthrough'. Socialism was everything or it was nothing. Without 'universal applicability' it was powerless. The argument for totality was later to have the reinforcement of continental theory, but it was already quite central in the platform set out in the opening editorial of *ULR* (spring 1957):

> Young people have defected from active political engagement, not because, as they sometimes say, 'there is nothing left to do' but because the tradition of socialist thinking failed to focus in any creative way on the gigantic problems which do, in fact, remain. Stalinism bred a fear whose consequence has been that whole areas of contemporary life have fallen beyond the reach of our 'political' commitment. Literature, art, our feeling for the quality of life and the community in an industrial society – these have all been consigned to some apolitical limbo. And the paradox is that when socialist values lose their relevance for the total scale of man's activities, they lose their 'political' point as well. They become expendable. Without universal applicability, socialism is open to the persistent erosive pressure from dogma and compromise: it is slowly nibbled to death.

The New Left believed that it was committed to industrial democracy. Although it was wary of 'workers' control' – a case for which was eloquently argued by Denis Butt in *NLR* – it followed closely the Yugoslav experience of workers' participation in management. But for all our denunciations of 'bureaucracy' and our well-advertised contempt for 'Morrisonian' nationalization (public corporations like the National Coal Board and British Railways) we were as committed to the idea of 'public ownership' as the most fundamentalist supporter of Clause Four. Indeed, we entered the lists on their side, publishing *The Insiders* as our contribution to the revisionist debate in the Labour Party, and setting up our stall at the Party Conference. Rogow and Shore's *The Labour Government and British Industry, 1945–51*, a scholarly study which showed – or was believed to have shown – that the nationalized industries had been subordinated to the needs of capital, was a text to which we referred continually. We entered into quite a close comradeship with one of its authors, who was then head of the Labour Party Research Department and later a Cabinet minister. 'Breathing isn't life,' wrote Ralph Miliband in *ULR* 7, 'but no one has yet found out how to have the one without the other. The same is true of nationalization and socialism.'

Our faith in planning was likewise undimmed, and article after article in *ULR* and *NLR* projected its extension into new spheres: now industrial organization, now education and the social services, quite often the arts, and most frequently the economy as a whole. A keynote article in *ULR* 1, reaching back to the planning of the 1945–51 Labour government and anticipating the gigantism of Harold Wilson's, was 'The Crisis in Town Planning' by Graeme Shankland, a recent ex-Communist who a few years later was to be the architect of the destruction of old Liverpool. It was the burden of his argument that 'piecemeal' slum clearance was a licence to anarchy, and that only large-scale redevelopment – undertaken 'in a great combined operation' and under a single directive intelligence – could prevent what he called the 'monotony of muddle'. *A Socialist Wages Plan*, a pamphlet which we published jointly with *The New Reasoner* in the run-up to the merger, was even more ambitious, proposing a national audit where differentials and relativities would be settled, the needs of the low-paid answered, and welfare norms imposed. 'Bureaucratic utopianism' according to one of its critics (Peter Sedgwick), and 'a constructive policy for . . . a period of planned economic expansions' according to its friends, this was to be our most influential contribution to Labour Party thought.

The weight of the past was particularly apparent in the New Reasoners who were, comparatively speaking, old political hands. Recruited to communism for the most part in the late 1930s or early 1940s, they prided themselves on their 'staying power', having survived the persecutions of the Cold War with their loyalties and beliefs intact. Ex-Communists, though of varying vintages – Doris Lessing seems to have left the Party in 1953, and Mervyn Jones at about the same period – they were above all determined not to succumb to the 'pathology' of anti-communism which had silenced so many erstwhile left-wing intellectuals in Britain and the United States in the McCarthy era. They argued for 'more fluid' interpretations of Marxism, but their basic confidence in it – and in themselves – was unimpaired. This was especially true of E.P. Thompson, though he had been perhaps the fiercest critic of Stalinism and moved furthest, in his intellectual loyalties, from anything which might be called Marxism. An almost Cossack sense of honour, refusing to yield an inch to enemy attack, and a fierce attachment to the vocation of the intellectual as an oppositionist, made him eager to proclaim himself a 'Communist', interpreting the term not as card-carrying membership of the Party but as commitment to the revolutionary idea. And in his early New Left writings, which appeared in both *ULR* and *The New Reasoner*, he was at pains to argue that communism had a humanist potential which needed only intellectual liberty to be realized. The struggle in 1956 was 'a struggle . . . for

Communism to regain its soul'.

In *ULR* the pressures to 'return to the fold' – to reaffirm a more traditional socialism – came from without rather than within, from the constituency of readers we discovered and the expectations which they entertained of us. Our older supporters and writers were typically veterans of earlier struggles and campaigns; the younger ones, such as those who came in large numbers to the London Schools Left Club, were often second-generation socialists, anxious to reaffirm or rediscover family loyalties. The editors themselves were very far from absolute beginners as far as socialist politics or beliefs were concerned. Although we may have aimed, ideally, to speak to the apolitical, we recruited our initial readership through the 'left' Labour journals of the day, *Tribune* and the *New Statesman*. We found ourselves increasingly drawn within the orbit of Labour politics, even though we had constituted ourselves as its fierce critics.

Our closest allies were with the Movement for Colonial Freedom, recently formed under the chairmanship of Fenner Brockway. The editor of *Tribune*, Dick Clements, was a good friend to us, as was Norman MacKenzie at the *New Statesman*. Anthony Wedgwood Benn made himself our ally when we attempted to mount a national campaign against the Algerian War; and we had an alliance of sorts with the 'Victory for Socialism' group, two of whose MPs, Stephen Swingler and Harold Davies, were kind enough to lend their names and their offices in raising funds for our Partisan coffee bar. With the publication of *The Insiders* we became embroiled in revisionist controversy in the Labour Party, taking sides as opponents of Mr Crosland.

For all our participation in extra-parliamentary agitation and our belief in the superiority of unofficial action and spontaneous 'movement' politics, we remained wedded to the idea that in Britain, Labour was the historically appointed vehicle for social change. By the time *New Left Review* was founded, in January 1960, we were deploying, editorially, a rhetoric of the 'labour movement', albeit in an oppositional sense, as readily as the career politicians who profited from it. For the New Reasoners the rhetoric had been there from the start, a carry-over from – or reach-back to – the British communism in which their politics had been formed. *ULR* was more hesitant and, though giving occasional coverage to strikes, left trade-union affairs alone. But as the merger approached it stepped into line, promising to 'develop, comment and work upon trade-union and industrial matters'. The opening editorial of *New Left Review* followed suit, promising to work 'through, between, around . . . the Labour Movement' while steering clear of its 'frozen monoliths':

What we need is a living movement of people, battering away at the problems of socialism in the mid twentieth century, pooling their experiences, yet, at every point, breaking back into the Labour Movement, thrusting forward like so many uninvited guests into Constituency Parties and Trade Union branches, pushing within CND . . .

Beneath such consciously socialist rhetoric, one might also discern what might speculatively be called a return of the socialist unconscious. It can be seen, for example, in the ways in which we reworked our theoretical innovations to assimilate them to traditional socialist categories. Thus the concept of 'alienation' was developed in a collectivist sense, to apply to a mass condition rather than, as in French existentialism, to individual isolation. Fashioned by Marx as a theory of labour in capitalist society, 'alienation' was used by the New Left to address the phenomenon of 'consumerism', to distinguish between 'true' and 'false' needs, spontaneous desires and manipulated ones.

'Alienation' involved a whole set of displacements in socialist thought. It transposed the two-camp division of society from the field of production to that of civil society. For the 'Mr Moneybags' of Marx's *Capital* it substituted such more indeterminate totalities as 'the mass persuaders'. As a concept it no doubt had a particular appeal to young people, speaking to a personal sense of dislocation. But we used it for a language of opposition rather than apartness, one which spoke in the name of the masses rather than defining itself against them.

A return of the socialist unconscious might account for the New Left's inabilities to speak on issues which turned not on social provision or collective action but, rather, on individual rights. For all our humanist rhetoric and spontaneous sympathy for liberationist causes, we remained conspicuously silent on matters of personal morality. On Home Office issues, as they were known at the time – for example the abolition of hanging, the radical revision of the divorce laws, the relaxation of censorship – we subscribed to the emerging progressive platform, but we never seem to have felt called upon to make any contribution to it, or to take up its agitation as our own. These issues were consigned, as it were, to some apolitical limbo.

Alan Lovell, one of our Oxford editors, had as a schoolboy been secretary of the Cardiff Campaign against Capital Punishment. Sydney Silverman, who was leading the abolitionist campaign in Parliament, was a very left-wing MP and his two sons, Paul and Julian, were part of *ULR*'s original Oxford circle. But neither *ULR* nor *The New Reasoner* contributed a line of advocacy to the cause. Again, Madeleine Simms, secretary of the National Campaign for Abortion Reform, was an active member of the London *ULR* Club, a member of our extended editorial circle and an occasional contributor to the *Review*, but there is not so much as a line of supportive argument in the two reviews. *NLR* praised 'frankness in the portrayal of physical love', one of the virtues found in the film version of *Room at the Top*, and was an ardent partisan of D.H. Lawrence. It did not, however, feel called upon to give space to the campaign against censorship – presumably because, as socialists, we had nothing distinctive to contribute to it.

It also seems that with the exception of an article attacking the 'aggressive femininity' of women's magazines in *NLR* 1, we had nothing to say about the family and women's rights. The near silence here may be explained, if not excused, by the fact that the left-wing politics of the time was gender-blind. Even so, the absence of take-up on Doris Lessing's *The Golden Notebook*, a milestone in British feminism written by one of our editors, gives rise to critical reflection.

More surprising is the silence on homosexuality which, in the wake of the Wolfenden Report, was the subject of major national debate. There were two homosexuals in our close circle and *ULR* was plainly fascinated by the phenomenon, even the glamour, of masculinity. Yet references to homosexuality are both exceptional and guarded – as in the reference to Geoffrey, the hero of Shelagh Delaney's *A Taste of Honey*, as a 'half queer'. Not until *NLR* 12 in December 1961, when the decriminalization of homosexuality was even agitating the Yorkshire Labour Party, is any space found for it in the pages of the *Review*.

Part of this deeply traditional imaginative complex was the idea of revival, a key term in the New Left lexicon. We cast ourselves in the role of the great awakeners, believing that socialism, in the last analysis, was *immanent* in the working class. We defined our project in evangelical terms: 'to stir up the dormant socialist traditions of this country', as E.P. Thompson put it; or, in the words of the New Left board when launching the merged journal, 'to propagate our socialist faith'. References to 'the fundamentals' of socialism are a leitmotiv of our appeals. The sense of rebirth was palpable at *ULR*'s opening, crowded meeting, with Isaac Deutscher, in an apocalyptic moment, prophesying the advent of 'the red sixties'. 'A young movement of ideas and people seeking to renew and rediscover the sources of their socialist conviction', was how the London *ULR* Club described itself in 1958. Stuart Hall, in the opening editorial of *NLR*, pressed on the religious analogy quite openly:

> The Labour Movement is not in its insurrectionary phase: we are in our missionary phase. The Left Clubs and the New Left centres – the New Left in general – must pioneer a way forward by working for socialism as the old missionaries worked as if consumed by a fire that is capable of lighting the darker places in our society. We have to go out into towns and cities, uni-

versities and technical colleges, youth clubs and Trade Union branches, and – as Morris said – *make socialists* there. We have come through 200 years of capitalism and 100 years of imperialism. Why should people – naturally – turn to socialism? There is no law which says that the Labour Movement, like a great inhuman engine, is going to throb its way into socialism or that we can, any longer – as the Labour Party does – rely upon poverty and exploitation to drive people, like blind animals, towards socialism. Socialism is, and will remain, an active faith in a new society, a faith to which we turn as conscious, thinking human beings.

Echoes of the thirties abound in the writings and *obiter dicta* of the New Reasoners; this was the time to which many of them owed their political formation. For E.P. Thompson it was exemplary: a time when ideas mattered, when intellectuals made common cause with the workers while yet retaining a proud sense of writerly or artistic vocation, a time when numbers put their lives on the line to fight fascism in Spain. It may be some indication of the depth of passion involved that Thompson's attack on W.H. Auden for his apostasy is the central passage in his contribution to *Out of Apathy*. His fellow-editor, John Saville, was hardly less committed to the memory of the thirties at the London School of Economics, that erstwhile bastion of student communism and the place where so many of the national liberation leaders from India and Africa sat at the feet of Harold Laski. The bond was shared with a younger member of the New Left board, Laski's sole remaining disciple at LSE, Ralph Miliband. One of their early joint projects was the mounting of a 'Harold Laski Forum' at the LSE; later, in the 1960s and 1970s, they were joint editors of *The Socialist Register*. Echoes of the thirties abound also in New Left projects: a large number of people were ready to see it as a 'movement of ideas' which would perform an analogous function to that of the Left Book Club in the time of the Spanish Civil War.

The *ULR* approach to the thirties was altogether more wary. Indeed, 'The Liquidation of the Thirties' was one of the articles announced in issue 1 (as the putative author, I might belatedly apologize for the fact that it was never written). Orwell, who did so much to shape our attitudes, may have cast some doubts on the thirties poets with his venomous references to the 'Nancy poets', and to Auden as 'a kind of gutless Kipling'. We were also much more uncomfortable than the New Reasoners with the title 'intellectual' and, as socialists who had supped on Tawney, were hardly enamoured with Laski as an exemplary socialist or with political science as a scholarly discipline. Nevertheless a thirties revival was a constant expectation of our supporters – even Isaac Deutscher who, as one who had been demonized by the Communists of the time, might have been expected to be critical of it, gave expression to

it. 'The Left in the Thirties' was the subject of an excited meeting which
we organized at the *ULR* Club, with Wal Hannington, the leader of the
unemployed workers' movement, and Philip Toynbee, the critic, as
speakers; we followed this up with an exhibition at the Partisan.

An alternative point of reference – which we kept well hidden even
from ourselves – was to Labour's victory in 1945. The New Left was too
proud and too left-wing to acknowledge any kind of debt to the Attlee
government. As a matter of honour, we could not identify with a
government which had waged colonial war, was the enemy of those of us
who had been Communists, and for the absolute beginners was an
example of corporatism and bureaucracy. Yet the strengths of the New
Left – or, at any rate, its distinctive character – were those of post-war
Labour idealism, of which it might be considered a late flowering. It may
be indicative of this that outside the bedsitterlands of W11 and NW3
our strongest local support came from the new towns. We had quite an
unproblematic belief in the virtues of education and a commitment to
developing it in democratic ways. We were on the side of the working
class, too, even though we did not make a great song and dance about
strikes; and did not doubt that socialism was a worker's faith even if,
under the influence of machine politics, it was fraying. Despite its revolutionary protestations, or posturings, the projects which really engaged
the enthusiasm of the early New Left had an unmistakably reformist
edge. Thus one finds the Glasgow New Left Club, within months of its
establishment, setting up a working group on technical education.

Typically, the New Left seems to have appealed to people who
wanted to get things done – supply teachers, shocked by the conditions
in the secondary modern schools; young architects, eager to see a more
generous use of planning powers; reformist trade-union officials,
anxious to see decision-making returning to the ranks. The Leicester
Experiment – the abolition of streaming by the city's education authorities – was the subject of one of our earliest public meetings, given
equal space and, I think, exciting no less controversy and attention than
such more exotic subjects as 'Russia After Stalin' or 'The Writer and
Commitment'. New approaches to English were the fundamental inspiration of New Left intervention in the schools; they found expression in a
number of practical initiatives, among them the founding of a National
Association of Teachers in English. Likewise the Notting Hill project,
started in the aftermath of the race riots of 1958: although it began as an
exercise in applied sociology, it took on the character of an authentic
and generously conceived Tenants' Defence League and branched out
into several initiatives: housing action against rack-renting landlords and
that early form of gentrification known as Rachmanism (the winkling
out of poor tenants in favour of rich buyers), the running of an adven-

ture playground and the formation of a community association. There was a reformist edge, too, to the New Left interventions in the arts, where 'Free Cinema' or 'Vital Theatre' were apt to be translated into community-based projects, most ambitiously through Arnold Wesker's Centre 42.

The New Left of the 1950s, by comparison with its later 1968 version, was thus quite moderate. It was also, in the manner of post-war Labour, paternalist. The secondary modern teachers and supply teachers did not doubt that they were missionaries or ambassadors of high culture, even if they interpreted their mission in oppositional ways and included ballads and songs alongside Burns and Blake. They were less concerned with democratizing structures than with setting up practical projects. They were concerned above all to be of use.

The relationship of the New Left and the old was a symbiotic one, complementary and antagonistic at the same time. The name seemed to carry the promise of a new start, yet the appeal – if the argument of the foregoing is accepted – was that of a revival of faith. We both resisted and drew from older traditions: on the one hand signalling new directions, on the other returning to ancient verities. Alert to the fragmentation and the emergence of new lifestyles, we nevertheless took a two-camp view of society as axiomatic, whether the point of comparison was the deprived and the privileged, the haves and have-nots, or the propertied and the propertyless. Our separation from the labour movement was more generational than ideological. It never ceased to be a primary point of reference – and ultimate court of appeal – even though many of us inhabited a different world. We drew on a common stock of collectivist beliefs; we shared – far more than we would have been prepared to recognize – a common metaphysic.

If socialism appeared to us unproblematical, this had to do less with its promise or practical achievements – on both of which (retrospection suggests) we were rather ill-informed – than with the fact that its historic enemies still seemed to be in place. Colonial wars were being fought in Kenya and Cyprus, Angola and Algeria; the Suez adventure suggested that the Tories were only too eager to turn the clock back; the Central African Federation, supported by the white settlers of Rhodesia, seemed to herald a new imperialist advance. In Whitehall the 'brass hats' of the army engaged in annual manoeuvres with the Admiralty to see that the military estimates went up. At Westminster the Cabinet was packed with Old Etonians, while behind the scenes the Marquess of Salisbury presided over the 'magic circle' from which the Tory leader emerged. In the City of London – a seemingly untouched aristocratic preserve rather than, as it is today, a staging post for international capital – the merchant banks and the insurance houses occupied (as we believed) the 'commanding heights' of the economy. The Church of England was still a pillar of the Establishment, and with an Archbishop of Canterbury who, as a member of the House of Lords, enthusiastically voted for capital punishment, it could still plausibly be represented as the Tory Party at prayer. The higher civil service, manned by classicists, was a cloistered elite, immune to the public gaze (the very idea of 'leaks' was then unheard of). The BBC spoke with a corporate voice. The Conservative Party, with an Edwardian gentleman at its head, seemed to enjoy a permanent electoral majority.

Our preoccupation with 'community', though greeted at the time as innovatory, also led us back to a two-camp – or two-nation – view of politics – which, at least for the young editors of *ULR*, seemed to have the more conviction because it drew its sustenance not from ideology but from lived experience. In a hugely influential passage by Richard Hoggart, drawing on his boyhood perception of Hunslet, Leeds, as well as on his political commitment, it was outlined in terms of 'Us' and 'Them':

> 'They' are 'the people at the top', 'the higher-ups', the people who give you your dole, call you up, tell you to go to war, fine you, made you split the family in the thirties to avoid a reduction in the Means Test allowance, 'get yer in the end', 'aren't really to be trusted', 'talk posh', 'are all twisters really', 'never tell yer owt' (e.g. about a relative in hospital), 'clap yer in clink', 'will do y' down if they can', 'summons yer', 'are all in a click (clique) together', 'treat y' like muck'.

In the case of *ULR*, which devoted four articles to Hoggart's *The Uses of Literacy* within months of its publication, it legitimated a return to class politics, albeit one based not on industry but on the solidarities of backstreet life. If the cultural struggle and the political were indivisible, it was because the hierarchical division between 'Us' and 'Them' seemed an organizing principle of British social life, however differently it might be perceived at varying points in the social spectrum.

Reference might be made, finally, to the moral capital accumulated by socialism in earlier times. For our comrades in the 'old' left, the reference was especially to the General Strike and the Labour pioneers. For Communists, it was to the October Revolution. Pre-eminent for the New Left was the much more recent phenomenon of the anti-Fascist resistance, a community of struggle in which numbers of our older collaborators had taken an active part and which provided us with our network of comrades in Europe. It served as an idiom of opposition bravely upheld in circumstances inconceivably more dire than any we were experiencing ourselves, yet one with which we had living links. It transcended the endemic conflict of rival left-wing political parties. It was uncorrupted by the exercise of power. It gave us a historic confidence not so much in the triumph of the socialist cause as in its essential justice. Curiously, since it was drawn from a memory of armed struggle, it went hand in hand with the common-sense pacifism of the Aldermaston marches. 'The Partisan' may seem an odd name to choose for a café in Soho, and references to the Resistance are few and far between in New Left writing, yet without the recent example of the Resistance I do not see how the idea of 'World Socialism' could have seemed a plausible project.

From the viewpoint of socialism, the New Left marked an end rather than a beginning. It came at possibly the last moment when a new politics could be thought of in terms of a resumption of Labour's forward march. Socialism was still – just – a workers' faith, the language not only, or even mainly, of political enthusiasts but of hundreds of thousands of Labour supporters, one more commonly encountered in doorstep canvassing or pub talk than in university seminars or espresso bars. In its Communist version it was still – before the Sino–Soviet split – an unbroken unity, advancing in South-East Asia even if its progress in Europe was stalled. In its social democratic version, in Britain and Northern Europe, it had transformed living conditions within a generation. More pertinently, it still seemed to have a whole reformist programme to fulfil. Above all, with two nations at work, two nations in health and housing, two nations at school, in a society where the ancient universities stood at a pinnacle of esteem and the Establishment was unchallenged, equality seemed an almost unattainable ideal. Whether conceptualized in terms of 'insiders' and 'outsiders' or high and low, the politics of the personal or that of public affairs, the struggle for equality seemed the very stuff of socialism, the point of juncture between our rather high-flown rhetoric and the felt inequalities of everyday life.

3

Marxism and Socialist Humanism

Charles Taylor

Rejecting as impoverished the two prevailing left doctrines of the 1950s, Stalinist communism and social democracy, the New Left sought to reconsider the basic moral and intellectual tenets of socialism. The ensuing attempts to spell out a 'socialist humanism' represent not so much a unitary theory as a shared set of concerns. Central among those concerns was an interpretation of socialism that put aside the rigidly determinist view of human beings as passive objects of historical processes and emphasized instead the idea that men and women are active subjects engaged in the creation of their social environment. 'All other forms of society have been suffered by men', wrote Alasdair MacIntyre in *The New Reasoner* 7, 'Socialism is to be lived by them.' This change of emphasis led to a growing interest in the early writings of Marx and in non-Marxist traditions such as that of British radical non-conformity.

Charles Taylor, one of the original contributors to this debate in the 1950s, reassesses his position on the extent to which Marxism itself can be seen to give rise to fundamentally anti-humanist forms of social organization. He reaches the provocative conclusion that socialists should abandon the Marxist paradigm altogether and search for an alternative theoretical framework in other strands of social and political theory. The questions and answers which followed his paper at the conference have also been included.

By humanism I mean some kind of doctrine about human potentialities which can command our moral admiration. The question is whether a socialist movement needs such a doctrine at all. This issue is raised today in a way it was not thirty years ago, in the writings of Michel Foucault and by post-structuralists. There is a movement on the left which thinks that humanist doctrines are an obstacle rather than a help, so the first issue I have to come to terms with is whether this kind of view about human beings is necessary at all or plays any role. I very strongly think that it does.

What I want to look at, therefore, is the role of moral ideas in left politics. The thought that it could function altogether without moral ideas is an illusion. This illusion is to some extent fostered by some variants of Marxism which have emphasized the notion of a 'scientific socialism', and also by such neo-Nietzschean movements of thought as post-structuralism and Foucault. Inevitably, this idea of functioning without moral ideas is an illusion. These movements always function with some moral ideas when they eschew humanism: they rely on some conception of justice or equality which they see as being violated. In other words, they function with a very strong sense of moral indignation against the existing order of things; that, of course, is very important and will always be an essential part of left-wing politics.

Nevertheless the danger of that being the entire spiritual food on which this movement feeds ought to be evident, because there is a kind of left-wing politics which turns into – and becomes largely motivated by – hatred and contempt: hatred and contempt, naturally, for the existing order, but also hatred and contempt for those who are identified as being part of it, and then hatred and contempt for all the people who are seen as not sufficiently opposed to it – which very often ends up including a lot of the people in the name of whom socialist movements have been launched. I think that one lesson from the long history of Marxism, Leninism, and Stalinism in particular is the degree to which this kind of hatred and contempt can become a major factor driving the people who are most active and take leadership positions in this movement, and the kinds of destruction to which this can lead. I believe that this kind of danger, and the way in which it can grow in left movements, was brilliantly – almost prophetically – described more than a century ago by Dostoevsky in a couple of his novels. That is what leads me to say at the beginning, as my first point, that a conception of human potentiality is an absolutely essential part of the spiritual background or basis of any left movement.

There is another type of danger that can arise from a humanism: a conception of human potentialities which is in important respects unrealistic. By that I mean that it does not face certain human limitations or negative sides of human beings. Very often the reason why doctrines of this kind have been popular is that people do not want to face these limits within themselves and therefore project them on to what they think of as 'the system', some impersonal structures existing in history, with the understanding that when these structures are overcome these limitations will no longer exist. The way this often enters the rhetoric of the left is for people to talk about 'the system' in some very impersonal way, as being at the origin of a series of evils or limitations that prevent people from having truly equal or truly brotherly relations, or from sustaining a self-governing polity, and so on. The problem is identified as some systemic element, and once this is overcome, the view is, these limitations will no longer affect us. They are not part of what it is to be human, they are part of some historically conditioned phase of the society and civilization through which we are living.

Paradoxically – or perhaps not so paradoxically – this kind of unrealistic humanism can end up generating the same kind of consequences as no humanist doctrine at all. In the face of the almost inevitable disappointments that people animated by this kind of humanism experience when they actually go into politics – and particularly when the movements with which they identify succeed – the same kind of hatred and contempt, for the ordinary people who are failing to live up to the consequences of the changes they have brought about, comes to the fore. I would argue that there is a certain underground affinity between a highly inadequate humanism of this kind and the flip-over into a neo-Nietzschean type of position which operates with no humanism at all. It can indeed look as though you are curing the problems and difficulties of an inadequate or overly optimistic humanism by flipping over into anti-humanist positions. This can be seen quite clearly in the case of Foucault: part of the defence of his position was built up against Marxism for having totally unrealistic expectations about the ways in which human existence could be transformed; he saw tremendously destructive consequences of this in Stalinism. That was one of the reasons why he felt justified in adopting an anti-humanist position. I mean anti-humanist not just as a curse word, but as the rejection of any kind of humanist doctrine.

So there are these dangers which stem both from a complete rejection of the humanist doctrine on the left, and also from a totally inadequate one. With this in mind, I want to start again the argument that we were in thirty years ago, but I shall express it in the terms that seem real for me today. This will, perhaps, be a rather skewed debate because I am going to be talking now about Marxism from this point of view, and I shall make a number of very harsh critiques of Marxism. The debate is also rather one-sided, because it is focused on Marxism. That was not inappropriate thirty years ago because Marxism was the major philosophical view on the left, and I suppose it still is not totally inappropriate today because, with the exception of the inroads made by these neo-Nietzschean movements, it probably still is the major intellectual, philosophical view on the left.

There are three criticisms I would make about Marxism. I shall make one very briefly and expand a little on the other two. I think that mainstream Marxism suffers from being an extremely inadequate humanism first of all because of its very unrealistic character. Classical Marxism, and Marx himself, seems to hold out the hope of an end to conflict. This arises from Marx's diagnosis of human opposition – that it comes from class society and class opposition, which in turn is something that originates in scarcity. So, by achieving abundance and by overcoming capitalist class society, these deeper inner conflicts can, at least in principle, be overcome. For a variety of reasons, I think that is an entirely unrealistic view. I am not going on further about this first point because many of the reasons for it will emerge in the elaboration of the next two points.

My second point is, in a sense, an elaboration of the first: there is a very deep flaw in Marx's theory of human sociality, his theory of the nature of human beings and human social existence. Any theory on the left has to come up with what I call a theory of social existence, simply because left movements occur in the context of modern capitalist societies with a certain culture: a culture within which a concept of atomism has become very deeply entrenched. By atomism I mean a picture of human identity in which human beings are conceived of as self-defining, self-responsible minds on their own, each as an individual with monological forms of thinking. What gets eclipsed here, however, is the way in which human beings are by their very nature part of social communities. We could not function as human beings without them, and any left movement has to recover the sense in which there is this 'social embedding' of human beings. There are different theories of this, and in particular different theories of how we can form part of self-governing communities.

Now what I want to do here is to sketch two models of the way in which we are social beings and the way in which that can form the basis of social self-government. The first one comes from Rousseau. Put very tersely, it is a view of human society as founded on a general will – that is, a common identity in which people can come together around a common purpose which is the goal that lifts them together into a single identity. This is what, of course, animated one important strand of the French revolutionary period – the strand that talked about one indivisible republic – and it is one model of our being social and having social purposes which can overcome the atomistic focus that normally comes to the fore in our culture and society.

There is a second model of human sociality which can be the basis for the self-governing rule of a community. As against Rousseau, I shall call it the 'civic humanist' model. Here I am gesturing at a tradition of thinking of which, for instance, Tocqueville is a major figure, and about which Hannah Arendt in our day has talked a great deal. This model makes us look at society as a participatory community in which the common institutions, the common rules and laws that give structure to the form of this participatory life, are seen as the common repository of the human dignity of all the participants.

The difference between these two models is the way in which they cope with the problem of conflict. In the second, civic humanist model, conflict and difference are far from being excluded. It is assumed that there will continue to be conflict, opposition, rivalry. As a matter of fact, the civic humanist model partly builds on actual experience, on the way in which the ancient republics and *poleis* were seen by their own members and by the philosophical tradition coming out of Aristotle. They are built on the idea that there will be continuing rivalry and conflict: rivalry for office and honours, conflict about interests, conflicts about ideas. And it looks as if the participatory society is a way in which the life of conflict, opposition and rivalry can also be a life which ensures the human dignity of the participants, because the terrain on which this conflict is carried out is one in which the participatory right of all the members is assured and the winning of the conflict has to take place in part through winning the supportive voice of the participants.

Now I would argue that the Rousseauian view emerges as the dominant view within Marxism. It emerges, of course, through a number of intermediary stages: through Kant, above all through Fichte (who, I think, is a more important figure for Marx than people usually believe), and then Hegel. The trouble with this model is that it takes over a conception of freedom from Rousseau, who in turn has taken over an atomist conception of freedom and then transposed it into society. The atomist conception of freedom is freedom as self-determination of or by the will: that is, I am free to the extent that I am not dependent on others but am determining the conditions of my own existence by my own decisions and actions. This becomes transposed into Fichte's idea of an almost total self-determination by the will. Marx then transposes it into a social form, in which the self-creating subject is no longer an individual but a social subject: the 'species being'. That is a very important change. The species being, in Marx's view, is the one that re-creates the conditions of its own existence, of human society as a whole. Let me call this the 'self-determining' notion of freedom.

As against that, in the civic humanist tradition freedom is defined as having a place in the ongoing order of political rule: there are certain framing common understandings, institutions and traditions which make that freedom possible. So freedom presupposes some things that are not entirely under the control of the common will. It presupposes the traditions, institutions and understandings which underpin this common participatory dignity. Freedom presupposes 'laws', as this expression is always used in the civic humanist tradition. So in one model of freedom the 'general will', to use Rousseau's term, remakes the conditions of existence, while the other conception of freedom presupposes something that has to be respected or allowed for outside this will.

There are two major reasons why this first view is inadequate, or even disastrous. Of course the number one reason, which was not evident in the nineteenth century but is terribly evident today, is that this view of freedom as self-determination is ecologically disastrous. The picture of human beings as having at their disposal a nature which has to be made over by the human will in order to serve human beings, and which otherwise poses no moral obstacle to the human will, is part of the deep problem with twentieth-century industrial civilization as a whole. It is one of the things that eggs us on towards continuing ecological disaster.

But this view is also disastrous in that it gives us the wrong understanding of political rule and freedom. It gives us a unanimist depiction of democracy: democracy and self-rule are attained when people achieve unanimous common will. Somewhere there is a real will that will unite all of us round it together. When conflict or disagreements occur, this is seen as an imperfection of the system that has to be overcome by further change, usually by steamrollering out the differences in order to arrive at this common will.

This is one way in which the inadequacy of not understanding, or not accepting, certain human limitations can turn out to be disastrous. The belief that the perfection of human freedom comes when there is some kind of unanimity is a crippling belief, and it is even more crippling because it encourages substitutionism and centralization. By substitutionism I mean the substitution of this putative real unanimous will which is somehow not yet agreed upon by the mass of the people, by the will of a vanguard minority. I am not trying to propose the simple hypothesis that Rousseau's philosophy itself, or Marx's development of it, leads to substitutionism: many other conditions have to arise for that to happen. But this unanimist conception of freedom and democracy opens the road to it by enabling a substitutionist politics to look good. Lenin, of course, is the major figure who set us on a path of substitutionist politics where a vanguard takes over in the name of the proletariat. Without some concept like the proletariat, as this concept is used in Marxist rhetoric – that is, a kind of super-subject to which one can impute a will or a direction of history in which, albeit unconsciously, it wants to move – the entire intellectual basis of a Leninist substitutionist politics would crumble.

The second feature of this model of democracy is a highly centralized notion: '*La République une et indivisible*'. People must express their common will through central institutions. This view is hostile to decentralization, because decentralization means that you carve out particular wills within the whole which can then come into conflict with other particular wills. And it is no accident that Lenin set his face very strongly in the very early years of the Soviet regime against the movements for workers' control that were rising in some of the trade unions.

I think Leninism is one of the great political disasters of the twentieth century – a great blight. By Leninism I mean this conception of the polity in which a vanguard minority not only seizes power but, more than that, sees itself as having the task of mobilizing the whole population towards some kind of transforming purpose. This class of regimes goes beyond those that are officially Marxist. It includes those regimes in the Third World which have modelled themselves on the Soviet, Chinese or Cuban experience. Leninism prompts such regimes to capture and make satellites of all the various movements or media in society that could potentially be foyers for self-organizing self-rule. In the extreme case of a totally organized Leninist regime even the chess federation becomes a Party satellite, and certainly the trade unions, the women's movement, and so on always suffer this fate. They never have any independent existence of their own but are always conveyor belts mobilized by the Party under its central leadership.

Now why is this a political disaster? Well, various things have happened. As a way of organizing and managing economic growth, centralism has some successes in the short term, but as we know, it is disastrous in the long term. In human and democratic terms it is a disaster because in my view, as a Tocquevillean, the health of citizen self-rule depends very heavily on the health of decentralized foyers of self-control. But not only have Leninist regimes stamped these out of existence, they have tended to forbid new ones to arise because, according to the model, everything has to be mobilized together by the Party. The struggle in Poland between Jaruzelski and *Solidarność* is just the most spectacular example of this: such regimes cannot live with the workers actually running their own lives. And the fear is that after seventy years of this in the extreme case of the Soviet Union, the political culture of self-rule has been so stamped out that it will be very hard to resuscitate, even if this huge weight were lifted.

Even without Leninism, it would be very difficult to get some kind of decentralized self-rule going in Russia again. Russia is a very difficult case because the catastrophe of Leninism occurred in a history in which there was previously the catastrophe of Ivan the Terrible, and it is probably not an accident that this history helped to lay the basis for Russian Leninism. Maybe, therefore, things are worse in Russia than they would be in the countries of Eastern Europe if this weight were lifted. Nevertheless, in the long term, it has a catastrophic effect on self-rule. It is a great engine of despotism. To sum up this second point against Marxism: in so far as this kind of humanism is built on the Rousseauian model, as against the Tocquevillean model, it is disastrous in the long run for democracy.

This brings me to my third criticism. The previous two points do not fully explain another extraordinary phenomenon of the twentieth century: the fact that between the Elbe and the Mekong Delta, Marxism is utterly spiritually dead. That is a slight exaggeration: I think there are people in East Berlin who hang on to a fragile belief in it and there are many, of course, who declare themselves to be officially Marxist. But Marxism is intellectually just about totally dead and it is eroded inside by time-serving and cynicism. Marxism somehow manages to live only where Marxist regimes do not.

How can one explain this? Well, it is partly to do with what I said earlier, but partly also with something deeper: the particular kind of militant atheist materialism that Marxism represents. When it comes to voicing a humanist doctrine, to defining the human potentialities that we hope socialist society may liberate, Marxism has too narrow a range. Beyond the potentialities for greater production and the domination of nature, what are they? They tend to be conceived in the Marxist tradition in terms of this self-determining notion of freedom. That is what

we shall see released in human beings, besides – indeed, on the basis of –
their control of nature in a Communist society. The problem with this
self-determining conception of freedom is that in a curious sense, it is
ultimately empty. It gives a picture of human beings as having this
tremendous potential to re-create themselves from out of themselves.
But just by turning within themselves, human beings end up having
nothing to say. It is not by looking inside that human beings give a
content to their lives in which they can believe and in terms of which
they can express their freedom.

Hegel's analysis in 'Absolute Freedom and Terror' in the *Phenom-
enology* aptly reveals the potential emptiness of this kind of freedom.
This kind of freedom can energize revolutionary elites for the task of
destroying the existing oppressive or limiting structures of their societies.
It powers the negative task of destroying and can also inspire a continuing act of supposed transformation under the aegis of the ruling
vanguard after the takeover of power. It can also lead to the persecution
of religion and other rival views. But it does not actually give a model
for what human life would be like to make it worthwhile, after all this
has been cleared out of the way. Now there you see a series of answers
that come to the fore when you ask this question of people or people ask
it of themselves: What will this free life be like?

Interestingly enough, going right back to Marx again, you find something else coming in at this point: images of artistic creation, of human
beings as artistic creators. There is a big question as to what Marx meant
here, and there are at least two doctrines that can be drawn out of
Marxism on this question about the relation of human productive potential to human self-fulfilment. One is the view that Marx sees the coming
of a Communist society as bringing about a state of affairs in which
productive labour will be reduced to a very small proportion of our time,
thanks to mechanization and abundance, and then the rest of human life
can be given over to more creative enterprises.

There is another view which sees, on the contrary, that productive life
itself becomes a kind of creative activity. What is wrong with capitalist
society, from that point of view, is the tearing apart of these two. But on
either of these interpretations there is a very interesting post-Romantic
conception in Marxism, according to which the definition of human self-
fulfilment and freedom after the overcoming of capitalism is to be seen
in terms of something like a life of artistic creation, extending through
great ranges of human life beyond the narrowly defined notion of art.
And it must be said that in 1956 this was part of the inspiration of the
original New Left which made us look at the whole range of human
culture in terms of its political dimension.

Now in the post-Romantic – I like to call it 'expressive' – age in which we have lived since 1800, artistic creation and artistic expression have been conceived of in two different ways. There are conceptions of artistic creation as self-expression and all sorts of people think of it in those terms – including, most recently, Habermas. It is that interpretation of artistic creation that moves it towards the model of self-determining freedom. On the other hand, there is a set of models in which what we are struggling to express is not ourselves, but something beyond ourselves. If you take the case of Rilke, for example, you find the view that poetic power is what enables us to say things about the world around us, or about the universe in which we live. I am leaving this vague simply because there is a whole disjunction of possibilities of what you might put there, but in any case there is an invitation to go beyond subjectivism.

My critique of Marxism is that it once more slides towards the self-expressive model, which I think is radically imperfect. I would say again, very dogmatically and for the sake of simplicity and brevity, that those parts of Modernist literature and art which have gone towards the self-expressive end of the spectrum have always become the more trivialized, shallower, less interesting; those which have gone towards the exploration or expression of something beyond us have been the deepest and most memorable.

Of course we can raise this, in a very broad sense, within the Marxist movement itself. Walter Benjamin, for instance, who thought of himself, for part of his life in any case, as some kind of historical materialist, is an example of the second kind of orientation I am thinking of. He sees the art and philosophy he is struggling for not in terms of self-expression but in terms of something beyond. Indeed, very specifically, he brings in theology and religion. That is the end of the spectrum for which I am strongly pleading today. Of course there are other people at that end of the spectrum who have thought of themselves to some degree as Marxists, for example Ernst Bloch. Although the situation is much muddier than I am describing it, my thesis is that if you go back to the actual doctrine of Marx, and if you take into account how that doctrine has been understood in its militantly atheist form by great numbers of people, you get a reading of that movement which has no place for the Benjamins and Blochs and which, therefore, tends towards the kind of sterility and spiritual death which I think has affected Marxism in its official position in the Soviet and Leninist world.

This is not to say that all kinds of materialism are being attacked here. If you look at the attempts to articulate something beyond us by people like Benjamin and others, you find that some of them do consider themselves materialists. It is a very mysterious area: there are theistic and non-theistic views here; there are materialist and non-materialist views.

There is a whole range of exploration going on in modern culture of the most important, fascinating and humanly meaningful kind, but it cannot survive in an atmosphere in which this whole dimension is negated by the wrong model of freedom. That is what I think you find in strictly orthodox Marxism, which is confident and dismissive of this dimension and therefore sterile. What I describe here as orthodox Marxism has really nothing to say about death, finitude, our relation to nature, and only shallow things to say about human distance or sin or moral transformation. That is why, as I said, from the Elbe to the Mekong Delta it is dead behind the eyes.

So those are the three criticisms. Maybe in the end the first did turn out to be a genus and the second two turned out to be species, and so maybe it is only two criticisms. What emerges from this positively is that we need (a) a kind of humanism in the socialist movement which can underpin really viable models of common self-rule which do not present us as impossibly unanimous angels but can actually accept – even, to some extent, affirm – the necessity of conflict and rivalry, but still have a conception of human dignity and common rule; and (b) a humanism which can allow us to explore this frontier of expression of the world, something beyond self-expression, and therefore another model of freedom. In these two crucial respects Marxism is terribly inadequate, and if we could free ourselves from it we would be much better off. All right, let me stop there, and let us talk.

Questions and Responses

Question 1: *Could I take you up on what one may call a very idealistic critique of Leninism on your part, in so far as this stultification of self-expression is concerned? I have two comments to make. First, when one criticizes Lenin for this stultification of self-expression one perhaps also has to place Leninism in the proper historical context: under what constraints was he propounding that particular line of thinking? Second, what is the alternative? Is it true, as you say, that there is no expression of self-determination in the wide area which we know as the socialist world? Is it true that we have humanism in the valley of the Thames, in what is called 'God's own country'? Is it true that we have humanism in a state where the first woman broadcaster loses her job because she has a Communist boyfriend? Is it not also true that in America people fighting against a nuclear war lose their tenured position, and so on? So is it not true that humanism itself has to be conceived within a specific class and cultural context rather than speaking of it in a broad, ideological, utopian sense?*

Taylor: I do not really see the relevance of that point because the remarks were mainly directed against the economy and policy of the USA, which I was not seeing as a model of socialist self-rule. We are looking for models of what it is to get beyond that. But if what getting beyond that means is any of the existing Leninist societies, then forget it.

First Questioner: *But then we have to forget humanism in the absolute sense. Where does humanism in the absolute sense survive except in the utopian, idealistic sense?*

Taylor: Well, where does it survive? Where is it in existence? If you mean, 'where is it integrally in existence', nowhere. But that is not necessarily an invitation to utopia because Marx himself had notions of human self-fulfilment which existed nowhere. We have to see what kinds of directions are possible from where it exists in fragments today. Now it exists more in fragment form in Western capitalist societies than it does in any Leninist society, because in many of these societies there are elements of self-rule which are extremely important and have to be built up. This is extremely important to point out. From the standpoint of socialist humanism, Leninist societies are in many respects way behind even capitalist societies.

Question 2: *I am speaking as a Marxist humanist and someone who has been influenced by the work of the late Raya Dunayevskaya. I would like to take up your understanding of Marxism and the Marxist tradition. My understanding of official Marxism, as opposed to Marx's own Marxism and to Marxist humanism, is that they are not just variants of the same thing but that they are absolute opposites. Marx's Marxism and modern Marxist humanism are a philosophy of liberation based upon the working class and the oppressed groups throughout the world, but official Marxism, as it is practised in Russia and China, is the ideology of a ruling minority in a state capitalist society, and a full counter-revolution and the Stalin purges and all the rest of it were necessary to bring that into being. Also, I do not believe that Marx had a view of freedom as unanimity, because one of the things not commonly recognized in Marx is his view of multilinear sources of revolution: he recognized not only the proletariat as a revolutionary force but also the Third World peasantry, just as he upheld the Taiping revolt in China, the Blacks in America, the slaves in abolitionism, and also welcomed the first stirrings of women's liberation in Europe.*

Taylor: Yes, Marxism is a philosophy of liberation, I entirely agree. I was too terse there. I did not mean at all to put humanist Marxism in the same basket in all sorts of respects as official Marxism, but just in this respect that I think that humanist Marxism still builds on that model of freedom as self-determination, and therefore still has a model of freedom which pushes towards both unanimism and this kind of emptiness. That is the problem. The humanist Marxists also have seen what is crippling in Leninism, or at least in Stalinist Leninism, and have very strongly protested against that, but I do not think that they have really developed a viable philosophical basis for an alternative in this important respect. This is not to say that any society based on that is bound to commit the crimes of Stalin – because some of those have to do with the particular historical circumstances in Russia – just that it will be lacking in the two respects that I described.

You are right, Marx did approve of certain movements and struggles. But as far as the Third World is concerned, he also thought it was a wonderful thing that the British were making India over in order to bring it to the point where the combined proletariat could overthrow capitalism. This is, after all, the underlying view. Anyone who says: 'We want to do it to liberate the working class' must be asked what lies behind that dictum: are you presupposing once again another super-subject in the working class or proletariat? If that is part of what is embedded in the logic of that kind of argument, we have the Rous-seauian model continuing at work.

Question 3: *One of the things that was at issue, as I recall the debate about socialist humanism in* The New Reasoner, *was the question of the sociohistorical conditions under which it is possible to be a moral agent, as well as what kinds of moral agent it is possible to be. Now you have mounted quite an effective critique of what is disabling in some kinds of Marxism and some kinds of political arrangements for fulfilling certain kinds of ethical arrangements. But what you left us with is nothing about what kind of ethical or moral constitution we have or might have, except rather vague references to the possibility of rooting them in some kind of religious doctrine. There is a kind of empty space in your critique which not only the socialist humanists in Britain in the fifties and sixties but also people like Sartre in France in the fifties and sixties tried to fill, seeing human beings as ontologically free and moral beings. I do not know where you are on that, and I should like you to comment on it.*

Taylor: There are two possible things that you might be getting at which I did not talk about. There is the very serious issue of working out an alternative model, which I gestured at in talking about Tocqueville. It is a model of self-rule which first of all not only allows for but takes for granted the existence of conflict and builds structures of self-rule on that basis. So one of the important differences that arises institutionally and structurally is that absolute priority be given to decentralized rule, because it is extremely difficult to sustain this kind of participatory self-rule in very large units – particularly if they are geographically spread out – unless it is also at the same time sustained in smaller units. This is a completely different model of democratic rule, a large part of which needs to be developed *de novo*. It was there in the tradition before and was somewhat rudely set aside by Marxism. Now, Sartre is no help in this regard because he took over some of the same conceptions.

Another thing which remains and has also to be taken up in socialist humanism is the picture of human beings as bearers of rights, which I do not at all want to set aside or consider to be simply a historical relic. What would be extremely interesting would be to go back over that whole tradition of thinking which generated both our conception of persons as bearers of rights and the crippling ideology of individuals as purely autonomous, self-responsible thinkers. These are two flowers from the same tree, but I think you can re-do the tree in such a way as to attain one of these and exclude the other. And the fact that it is extremely important to do this is also implied in your question, because one of the things swept aside by this unanimous general-will tradition is this very strong notion that human beings are bearers of rights over and against any society: Rousseau classically says that the society of the general will should not reserve entrenched rights to its component individuals. So I take these two points very strongly.

Question 4: *I should like to ask a question about a socialist society. Poland is a nation where you could see the problem of cultural and national identity worked out throughout the nineteenth century. I am wondering how nationalism, Marxist critiques of it, and internationalism fit in with your idea; whether, in your model, we can really talk about socialism on an international scale, or whether it becomes, say, socialism on the scale of a church choir.*

Taylor: Part of the conditions for self-rule as we see it historically is some very strong sense among participants of their common institutions as a repository of their common dignity, so you cannot just take any group of people chosen at random and expect them to maintain institutions of self-rule. There has to be that common bonding. Now, for better or worse, one of the most powerful forms of common bonding in the twentieth century is nationalism. This is not an accident, but has to do with the development of a modern identity. And it would be completely utopian (in the bad sense) to think that we could move towards socialist self-rule, at any case in many countries of the world, completely ignoring or trying to neutralize nationalism. That, of course, creates the very real danger of chauvinism, but there is no way round this simply by negating nationalism altogether. In certain societies it is going to be a very important part of the mix.

Question 5: *I have two questions. First of all, you seem to be implying that there is a form of atomism in Marx's writings. I find this quite surprising, given his notion of man as the ensemble of social relationships and his critique of rights in 'On the Jewish Question'. The other problem which your talk raises is whether or not you can both celebrate conflict as a potentially liberating force, and at the same time reject this atomistic concept of the person as self-determined. To some extent the two have gone together in the past.*

Taylor: I did not say that Marxism is a kind of atomism. What I said was that the model of freedom as self-determination is a model that originally arises out of atomism and is then transposed on to a social subject by Marx so that it is no longer an atomist view. It is a theory of freedom of a social subject: that is the only link. Historically, this conception of freedom as self-determination was evolved out of atomistic conceptions.

On your second point: I think we do have this other historical model, going back as far as Aristotle. He gives a picture of *polis* rule predicated on the idea that people are rivals for offices and honours, but here the rivalry is understood to be fought out in a way that continually entrenches a set of laws and rules which respects the dignity of the members. That is a model which existed before atomism, and it can exist after. The terrible thing about the freedom-as-self-determination model is that it leaves you with only two possibilities: atomist conflict or the total suppression of conflict by unanimism.

Question 6: *I just want to make a moderate defence of Marxism against some of your charges. It is one thing for a person to say: 'I affirm the main claims of Marxism', and another for a person to say: 'I believe that all the important claims that can be made about human beings and society are identical with the main claims of Marxism.' It is one thing to affirm Marxism, and another to say: 'The only important and valuable thing worth affirming is Marxism.' I do not think Marx affirmed the second, but the Stalinist element of the tradition certainly came to think that the answers to all important human questions are to be found in Marxism. Yet there are important indications in Marx to the contrary. In the 1859 Preface to* A Critique of Political Economy *– which could be said to have an apocalyptic resonance in a way that serves the purposes of the kind of characterization you want to offer – he says that with the* *proletarian revolution against capitalism the prehistory of human society comes to an end, and antagonism between people comes to an end – but, he then adds, antagonism not in the sense of personal antagonism. This strongly implies that personal antagonism on all kinds of bases persists, but in the sense of antagonism rooted in the material conditions of life. Now it seems to me that antagonism between social groups which is rooted in the material conditions of life is a transcendable circumstance, while personal antagonism is not, and I think that much of the subsequent deformation and Manichaean sort of paranoid approach to politics you are talking about did obtain. So I think you are right about the phenomenon, but you look for its seeds too much in Marxism itself and not enough in the false and unnecessary belief that Marxism pronounces on all the important questions there are.*

Taylor: I still think that Marx is more deeply embedded in that than you, partly because the very idea which you attribute to Marx makes sense only if you have this kind of unanimist view. Why should we think that antagonism rooted in the material conditions of life should ever disappear? Imagine a society in which all the means of production are owned in some social form – nationalized industries or workers' control, or the Yugoslav model, or co-operatives – and imagine those engaged in export trade versus those engaged in local markets, those interested in this region's development versus those interested in that region's development. There will be policy differences interwoven with these kinds of antagonisms. Typically, there will be some mix of policy differences based on different views of the general good but alimented by concrete differences of interest.

Sixth Questioner: *Antagonism is a strong word, isn't it?*

Taylor: But the whole diagnosis which comes out of Marx, and which attributes the deep conflicts in present societies simply to this particular form of material base, implies that once we get over this particular type of class society those deep conflicts will no longer exist, and this seems to me very unrealistic. But apart from that, it would make sense only on the supposition that some very strong unanimous purpose will arise out of the suppression of this particular base, thereby making unnecessary or nonexistent further conflicts of this kind. That is why I think that we probably do not disagree about a large part of the tradition that comes out of Marx, but that we are disagreeing about Marx himself.

Question 7: *I totally agree with your condemnation of the outgrowth of Marxism, but I totally disagree with your diagnosis. What led to these* *perversions was not that the idea of a self-determining subject was taken too seriously, but that it was denied. What is dangerous is not the absence of any transcendent doctrine, but precisely the idea in Marxism, as in Hegelianism and Christianity, that there is something we have to aspire to which goes beyond our well-understood needs and interests. It is not individualism but the denial of individualism that has led to Leninism.*

Taylor: This question is very deep and challenging, and it's a very important strand of modern moral thinking: if only we could get away from these immense spiritual aspirations to some higher perfection, we would take away from ourselves the source of all our self-persecution and hence other-persecution. Now, I think that is both tremendously insightful and deeply wrong. We probably agree on the insightful part of it, but what is deeply wrong about it is that it completely misreads what human beings are like. This deep hunger exists in human beings and is never going to be stilled in them. The attempt to do without it is just like whistling in face of the wind. There are these profound aspirations in human beings which come out regularly in great programmes of reform as well. It is not an accident, it is not an excrescence; it has got to be taken to be there, and we have to come to terms with it sometime and find a human form for it. The idea of turning our backs on it would make as much sense to me as someone who says: 'Look at all the sexual hangups that people have in the universe, let's do without sex.' I say, good luck to you! That would be my answer to that.

Question 8: *I would like you to elaborate on the possibilities of this kind of civic humanism in the modern world, given that the other humanist you mentioned, Hannah Arendt, is clearly very pessimistic about that possibility.*

Taylor: I am not wildly optimistic either. Also, in a Tocquevillean-type programme, there are no general formulae, because such an approach puts an important emphasis on the traditions that bind people together. So the prescriptions for having a human society will be different in different areas. But at least in some societies in the world today, those that are not hyper-unified or hyper-centralized, there are these kinds of breakdowns, partly regional, where people can identify with institutions not coterminous with the entire society. There might also be some traditions of self-management in the form of co-operatives. A society in which a number of these developments come together might realize something like Tocquevillean decentralization. There are other societies in which the things I have just mentioned do not seem to be there, and I do tend to get very despairing when I think of those societies. But perhaps the people living in those societies might be able to see possibilities I cannot see.

Question 9: *My question is also about the role of conflict in socialist humanism. You seem to be gathering many kinds of antagonism under this category of conflict. What I am curious about is, first, where these conflicts come from. You are assuming that there are certain kinds of conflicts that are always going to be there. I think that for the programme to be credible you need some characterization of why there are such conflicts and what it might take to resolve them. Part of the problem seems to be that you have a tendency to subtract these political institutions from everything else that is going on in people's lives – most obviously, in the context of Marxism, from the economy. The relationship of political institutions to everything else seems to me very important. Second, what happens if, in the course of discussion within an institution, there arises a conflict which threatens the very basis of that institution, so that the conflict becomes irresolvable within that institution?*

Taylor: I am thinking of these political institutions very much as being embedded. I have some vague image in the back of my mind, like Alec Nove's picture of feasible socialism. But in that kind of society, which I think really is feasible, there are still the following kinds of bases for human conflict. First of all, there remain deep dilemmas – dilemmas that Marxism, and Marx himself, did not take enough account of: for instance, between the exigencies of market relations on the one hand and the exigencies of common planning and common purposes on the other. Those standing dilemmas mean that people are going to distribute themselves on different sides of the issues. Woven into that will be, secondly, the fact that people will have concrete interests which will also, combined with the first source of conflict, link them to one horn of the dilemma or the other. One horn will be less uncomfortable for me than it will be for you, and that will have something to do, perhaps, with our taking the stand we do on the dilemma. Thirdly, there will be tensions because of the nature of our common identities, be they national or linked to existing historical communities: sometimes between states, but sometimes within states. Of course, I come from Quebec, a society where that is extremely evident. This kind of tension between groups and nations will go on, and all these and others will be woven together. It seems that one can very much foresee them existing because of the nature of the society and because of the nature of the economic system, not at all abstracting from it, and I see no conceivable regime which can do without at least the three kinds of sources of conflict that I have just described. I think that would be utopian in the bad sense. Now, even within this kind of regime there could arise conflicts so deeply felt as to be unresolvable, particularly national ones. Two nations might find it impossible to live together in the bosom of a single state, and then you break it up. There is no guarantee in history against that, certainly not socialism.

4

Resisting the Cold War: Positive Neutralism and Non-alignment

Reacting to the threat of nuclear war as well as to the Anglo-French takeover of the Suez Canal and the Soviet invasion of Hungary, members of the New Left argued for a foreign policy of 'positive neutralism'. While actively supporting the Campaign for Nuclear Disarmament they called, more radically, for the abandonment of bloc politics and for Britain's more positive engagement in the non-aligned movement. The realization of self-determination in the international sphere implied an end to imperialism and, for the newly decolonized and other non-aligned nations, an adequate economic and political space in which they could find their own paths of social development.

Michael Barratt Brown examines the New Left's proposals for planned international trade and emphasizes the necessity of linking economic co-operation and disarmament. Peter Worsley concentrates on the political aspects of positive neutralism and highlights the importance which the New Left attached to the newly independent 'Third World'. Both stress the continuing force of these ideas and the continued need to support struggles for emancipation throughout the world.

Positive Neutralism
Then and Now

Michael Barratt Brown

The Reasoner first appeared in July 1956 and *The New Reasoner* and *Universities and Left Review* in spring 1957. 1956 was the year of the Khrushchev revelations and the defeat of the Hungarian uprising on the one hand and, on the other, of the defeat of the Anglo-French attack on Suez and the beginnings of African decolonization. These events released the previous straitjacket of the two camps in which our thinking about world problems had been confined. There had already been some loosening a year earlier: after Khrushchev's visit to Tito in 1955 and his disavowal of Beria, polycentrism in the international Communist world seemed possible; and after the meeting at Bandung of representatives from twenty-nine African and Asian states, including China and India, a 'Third World' emerged as a non-aligned third force in the world. We were already beginning to live under the shadow of the H-bomb, and we were looking for a way out of a threatened nuclear arms race.

I should give a central place in the early thinking and activity of the New Left to our commitment to the campaign around the bomb, not only to CND but also to the concept of positive neutralism, which has an economic as well as a political content.

Positive Neutralism

Especially for those of us who had failed to shift the British Communist Party away from its support for the Soviet Union over Hungary and had subsequently left the Party, non-alignment was the natural recourse. After Khrushchev's revelations and despite the invasion of Hungary, it seemed likely that Khrushchev could introduce a more open regime in the Soviet Union and replace the overcentralized command economy with a more decentralized system of self-managed enterprises. The Liberman Reforms of the early 1960s seemed to show the way for a new stage of economic development in the Soviet Union, just as the Cultural Revolution did in China. But while we looked to the Communist bloc as important trading partners, we did not see Comecon as the right framework for Britain's economic development. Still less were we likely to turn to the Atlantic Alliance. The emergence of a non-aligned group encouraged us to seek ways of linking Britain to it. By 1960 most of the British and all the French colonies in Africa had become independent, and so had most of the colonies in Asia. There appeared to be new national populist governments in India and Egypt, Ghana and Algeria, Brazil and Indonesia which were planning their economies so as to raise the standard of living of ordinary people. By trading with them we could create space for their own development and for our movement towards socialism.

At the same time, the Treaty of Rome establishing a European Common Market was signed in March 1957, and the pressure was on Britain to join what seemed like a West-end European capitalist club, tied firmly to the American alliance through NATO. Although Britain had been in NATO since its inauguration in 1949, economically it was part of the European Free Trade Area – apart from Britain a basically neutralist group of Scandinavian countries with Austria, Switzerland and Portugal. The United States regarded this neutralism as incompatible with membership of the Atlantic Alliance, and the Labour Party was deeply divided between Atlanticists and Neutralists. The New Left threw itself wholeheartedly into supporting the latter and was the first to reveal the links between the CIA and writers in *Encounter* who formed the Campaign for Democratic Socialism to fight unilateralism in the Labour Party. (Much later this campaign became the core of the SDP.)

The role of the New Left in swinging the Labour Party vote behind unilateralism at the Scarborough Conference of 1960 should not be underestimated. The New Left clubs' discussion had paved the way and the daily briefings prepared by the New Left editorial staff provided a formidable bombardment on delegates' thinking. The vote was over-turned by Gaitskell with the aid of the Campaign for Democratic Socialism at the next conference at Blackpool and the way was opened for Britain's entry into the Common Market. The two questions of nuclear disarmament and an alternative to the Common Market were brought together in a series of articles I wrote for *The New Reasoner, ULR* and *New Left Review* and in a New Left pamphlet I wrote with John Hughes in 1961, as well as in articles and a New Left pamphlet by John Rex.

But we did not stop at articles and pamphlets. In 1962 and again in 1963, we supported a so-called Britain–EFTA–Commonwealth Conference to argue not only that Britain should stay out of the Common Market but that a World Economic Conference should be called to provide the alternative that so many in Europe and in the non-aligned countries were seeking. These London conferences attracted a wide range of participants, including leading trade unionists, prominent Labour Party members, Conservatives, and Keynesian economists. But we failed to influence in any way the policies of Harold Wilson when he became Prime Minister in autumn 1964, and it is necessary for us to examine that failure if we are to learn lessons for today.

What Went Wrong

First, our analysis started from the close links that our studies had revealed between the City of London, British industry at home and overseas, and the nationalized industries. In these linkages the most obvious element fully recognized by British industry was the strength of the government's position. State expenditure had risen by 1968 to 45 per cent of the national product; public-sector employment accounted for 25 per cent of the total. (Even after the Thatcher cuts these shares were not much changed, despite the growth in the number of local-authority employees.) Until 1979 the main field of capital investment was the home economy, and exports of goods had been raised by the 1960s so that they roughly balanced imports at a level of about a quarter of the national product. It was the growing gap in this balance of payments that caused Britain's crisis in the 1960s, and we missed the implications for the growth of trade inside the transnational companies when the Wilson government hesitated to use the power it had to manage the economy.

Second, our proposals to solve Britain's crisis were based on a much greater element of economic planning under a new Labour government than had existed since 1948. A key part of this was to introduce an element of planning Britain's international trade – not through submission of the trade to any international authority but by a system of international agreements for expanded trade exchanges with other countries planning their economies, this system to be subject to a clearing arrangement similar to the post-war European Payments Union. As it transpired, Labour did introduce a National Plan, but it was ill-conceived, had no support from the Treasury, and collapsed precisely on the failure of exports to grow in line with imports when home demand rose.

Third, the dynamism of the German and Japanese economies after the destruction of the war quite changed the balance of world economic power. Britain and EFTA accounted in 1959 for some 15 per cent of world exports, as did the USA; Germany for 8 per cent and Japan for 3 per cent. Twenty-five years later the USA, Germany and Japan each account for 10 per cent, the UK and EFTA for only 9 per cent between them.

Fourth, the expectation of continued rapid growth of the economies of the Communist countries proved very wide of the mark. By extrapolating growth rates between 1948 and 1959, we expected that the share of USSR, Eastern Europe and China in world trade would grow from 14 per cent in 1960 to over 30 per cent in 1975. In the event, it fell to 10 per cent.

Fifth, and most serious, the links through the Commonwealth with the Third World were to be forged via the new national populist ex-colonial regimes that had declared their non-alignment with either of the two blocs. Within less than a decade of the Bandung meeting, Nehru was dead and the CIA had effectively assisted in the overthrow of Sukarno in Indonesia, Nasser in Egypt, Ben Bella in Algeria, Nkrumah in Ghana, Goulart in Brazil. Only Tito remained, and Yugoslavia was forced to come to terms with the European Community in order to replace the lost opportunities for trade exchanges in the Third World. It was this premature opening of the Yugoslav economy to the West, combined with the decentralization of power to the separate federal republics, that destroyed the successful development of a decentralized planned economy in Yugoslavia as well as its attempts at industrial democracy.

Sixth, it is necessary to add to this tale the divisions inside the New Left over its relationship with the Labour Party. The stance which Stuart Hall describes as 'one foot in the Labour Party and one foot outside' was not likely to encourage the Party to listen to New Left advice, especially when some members of the New Left supported independent candidates against party candidates in elections.

Seventh, I feel bound to add that we often appeared, except in the practice of writing and the arts, like a bunch of amateurs. We could not even run a coffee bar without losing money – how much less could we be trusted to manage the country's foreign trade! This lack of managerial skills became more obvious than ever when the Greater London Council and some other Labour authorities set up enterprise boards to manage business enterprises. The lessons have still not been learned. As yet there is still no Labour management college, nor even courses in management at the trade-union colleges. This is all the more surprising because the main bequest of the New Left to the Labour movement was certainly in the field of education. It was not by chance that many of us involved were tutors in the Workers' Educational Association, in university extramural departments and polytechnics and in the residential colleges. This is where we forged links with shop stewards and the trade unions – links that became most evident in the conferences, publications and actions of the Institute for Workers' Control.

Conclusions and Prospects

There is little value in rehearsing these prospects and arguments of thirty years ago if we do not suggest what lessons may be learned from them. The situation today in many ways resembles that of thirty years ago, although there are also major differences. Britain has been part of the European Community for fifteen years, and proposals for world trade expansion must be made through the Community and not apart from it. Japan and West Germany are now challenging the USA for economic hegemony. At the same time, the prospects for rapid economic advance in the Soviet Union and in China look better than for many years. India and Brazil are now major industrial powers, though burdened with great debts. What *is* similar to thirty years ago is the urgency of a solution to Britain's economic crisis. For whatever Nigel Lawson may say, as the oil revenues run down Britain's balance of payments dips sharply into the red. All the income from the last decade of investment overseas will not be enough to cover the failure of British manufacturers to compete with imports from all over the world.

I am still convinced, however, that our proposals for positive neutralism indicated the best road to follow for the British people. An essential element in the concept of positive neutralism was always the development of planned international trade exchanges between like-minded states in what came to be called the First, Second and Third Worlds. Nothing came of the proposals we made in the 1960s, although they were taken up at different times in United Nations assemblies. Most governments withdrew from planning their trade and concerned themselves with problems of managing interest and exchange rates, a purely negative role that did little to encourage an expansion of trade exchanges except those within the giant companies.

It was sometimes said in criticism of our proposals for planned trade that they would only perpetuate the unequal and artificial division of labour between the rich and poor countries and would not end the exploitation of poor peasants, plantation labourers and mine workers. We did not say it would, and I would not claim that now. I would say only that through planned trade there is some chance for Third World countries to diversify their economies. What our ideas pointed to then and point to now is no more than the creation of a space – first, for us all to survive: second, for the peoples of all parts of the world to find their own solutions to their social development. Without a new framework for international economic co-operation, that space does not exist. It cannot be too often repeated that the ordinary people of the developed countries do not benefit from the impoverishment of the underdeveloped. Some who own shares in transnational companies may benefit, as will others who can retain their jobs while falling prices of imports from the Third World raise their real wages. But this is at the expense of increasing numbers of unemployed and greater economic insecurity for all in the developed world, not to mention the greater threat to world peace.

What is new today is that a number of Third World countries, apart from China, have begun to build socialism on the basis of national liberation struggles – Cuba, Vietnam, the ex-Portuguese colonies, Zimbabwe, Nicaragua, Eritrea. Despite all the hangovers of past corruption and elitism and the continuing presence of giant transnational companies they are looking eagerly for alternatives to the transnationals, both for marketing their products and for obtaining the capital equipment they need for their development.

Even within countries where new class formations have not yet succeeded in challenging their capitalist rulers, regional and city authorities, especially in Latin America, and peasant associations and co-operative federations throughout the Third World are looking to establish similar alternative channels for trade and technology to flow along. There is a proliferating network of twinning arrangements between towns, cities and regions in the First, Second and Third Worlds that have gone beyond purely ceremonial functions to involve the exchange of goods and services. Thus a conference organized recently by the charity of which I am the chairperson, Third World Information Network (TWIN), designed to bring together organizations which had established joint actions for equal exchange in trade and technology transfer between the First and Third Worlds, attracted representatives from fifty Third World countries and twenty in the First and Second.

It has been an important experience for me to have to put into practice the rhetoric of those last paragraphs of my books about creating a truly fraternal framework for co-operation between workers in the First and peasants in the Third World. What we are doing in TWIN is still on a minuscule scale compared with the operations of the transnational companies, but it offers an alternative to hard-pressed governments in Nicaragua and Mozambique and can become a prototype for a new international economic order.

The development of closer economic co-operation also provides the necessary underpinning for nuclear disarmament. The prospect of a major move towards nuclear disarmament today recalls the time when the first ban was agreed on testing bombs above ground. This first check to the nuclear arms race did not lead to any real detente – and I would argue that this was because it was not associated with any moves towards economic co-operation. We cannot afford once again to fail in linking military, political and economic solutions.

So great are the numbers of workers and other resources involved in the arms race that conversion is an issue of the greatest importance which will require the most careful advanced planning. As I have suggested, a major weakness of our thinking in the 1960s was our lack of detailed management skills. Fortunately, we now have some small experience: of workers' corporate plans like those of the Lucas Aerospace shop stewards and local enterprise boards, of the new generation of workers' co-operatives, and of the charities operating in the Third World like Oxfam, War on Want, Traidcraft, and TWIN. Today, Gorbachev has seized the initiative in suggesting a link between disarmament and development that should be realized in actual exchanges of civil products between First, Second and Third World countries to replace the arms trade. The Bertrand Russell Peace Foundation has responded to this initiative by setting up a programme of joint studies with the Soviet Peace Committee on the technical problems of arms conversion. After more than thirty years of total alienation from the Soviet regime, I am happy to be engaged in this work and look to my New Left comrades and others to join me in the endeavour.

Non-alignment and the New Left

Peter Worsley

Before 1956 political thinking of all varieties was dominated by the assumption that the world was divided into two blocs, and by the belief that the superpowers were the only significant forces in global politics. The conjuncture of Suez and Hungary destroyed overnight the two dominant myths which had hitherto been used to justify the competition for world hegemony: the ideology of Western liberalism and the ideology of Stalinism. We rejected both ideologies; in their place we asserted the principle of self-rule – a principle which is still valid, even in a changed world.

Many of the key ideas of the early New Left were not necessarily original, but revivals of older socialist traditions from Robert Owen to the Guild Socialists. The work initiated by the early New Left – in writings such as *The Insiders* and *The Controllers*, about the undemocratic nature of capitalist ownership and control – drew upon classic socialist ideas about the need for self-rule by the producers themselves, rather than rule by politicians and technocrats. Running through the ideas of the New Left was the theme of the emancipation of human capacities. For us democracy meant not just the ballot box but participation in decision-making at all levels, not just at work or at the level of national institutions but in all spheres of everyday life.

In a Europe where the Cold War was the central danger, any political potential for self-rule meant rejecting categorically the notion, expressed most influentially by *Encounter*, that the only choice open to humanity was the choice between Washington and Moscow. The neutralism of the New Left was not merely a negative critique of bloc politics, nor the Swiss–Swedish liberal kind of neutralism (which never makes judgements about international conflicts, only about profits). It was a *positive* neutralism, aiming at the creation of a political space in which, globally, superpower hegemony could be dismantled and colonized peoples could free themselves – the prerequisites for ending world poverty and abolishing the bomb. For us in Britain, it meant a new opportunity to align ourselves with movements for self-determination all over the world.

In Europe the New Left looked to Yugoslavia, which had broken politically with the USSR and had also rejected that country's reliance upon centralized, *dirigiste* economic planning as the *sine qua non* of socialist economic development in favour of what were to become very influential experiments in workers' control. French socialists also tried to develop a position independent of both the Stalinist French Communist Party and the Gaullist right. (See, for example, the Summer 1958 issue of *The New Reasoner*, and other New Left contributions such as John Rex's *NATO or Neutrality* [Young Fabian pamphlet, May 1961] and Stuart Hall's *Steps Towards Peace* [1963].)

The convergence of neutralist elements in Eastern and Western Europe necessarily involved common resistance to the superpowers' military apparatuses – NATO and the Warsaw Pact – and to the major instruments deployed by the two blocs – nuclear weapons. *The New Reasoner* quickly threw itself into the new Campaign for Nuclear Disarmament. Within a short time, the leafleting of Central London for the 1958 Aldermaston March was being organized by Raphael Samuel from the offices of *Universities and Left Review* in Soho.

The extraordinarily difficult task of trying to build a common front against nuclear war, despite the division of Europe, began in the very first issues of *The New Reasoner*, with a particularly important input from Edward Thompson. Today I think we can say that that struggle has borne fruit in the form of the Europe-wide association of mass and active national movements that make up European Nuclear Disarmament, and that the New Left played an honourable and not insignificant part in the process.

But resistance to nuclearism was, at that time, far more widespread outside Europe. In the late fifties and early sixties the Third World was thought of as a vital new force in international affairs, challenging the hitherto unchallenged hegemony of the superpowers. At independence, most of the new states wanted to maintain a healthy distance between themselves and both superpowers. The Indonesian leader Sukarno, for example, urged that the 'newly emerging forces' should constitute themselves into an organization which could rival the United Nations, which was seen as dominated by the developed world and in particular by the superpowers. It was, however, Nehru's view – 'if a neutral nation joins a neutral bloc, it ceases to be neutral' – that won out.

The colonies which won their independence used their new-found

power to assist others to win theirs. Kwame Nkrumah, the leader of
Ghana, hosted several major All-African conferences aimed at inspiring
independence movements in other areas of Black Africa. Patrice
Lumumba went straight back home from one of them to launch the
independence struggle in the Congo. Nkrumah also brought European
anti-nuclear and anti-colonial activists to Ghana to oppose the French
nuclear testing on the soil of its colony, Algeria, where there was armed
revolution. The basic assumption that had governed world politics since
1945 – that the only significant agents of history were the superpowers –
was therefore thrown into question overnight.

We aligned ourselves squarely with these movements for national
liberation: John Rex attended one conference in Ghana on behalf of
CND, while I went for the New Left, and Stuart Hall went later. Tom
Mboya, Kenneth Kaunda and Kanyama Chiume wrote for *The New
Reasoner.* Both John Rex and I regularly appeared on anti-colonial plat-
forms in this country, as did Doris Lessing.

It is all too easy, in retrospect, to see that we were overoptimistic
about the future course of the Third World states and that we over-
estimated their degree of autonomy. Increasingly in debt to the West,
these new states were eventually forced to conform to the requirements
of donor countries and foreign-owned international institutions. The
replacement of the original socialist nature of some of the projects did
not come about because of the dictates of a redesigned global manufacturing system, as economistic models would have us believe. It called
for an act of political will on the part of world capitalism: the destabil-
ization and removal of radical and progressive regimes, especially by the
CIA.

Third World countries tried hard to avoid embracing either bloc.
Over the intervening quarter-century, in fact, there has been a steady
growth in the number of countries adhering to a deliberately loose non-
aligned grouping. This grouping has come to include the great majority
of Third World states, which together have enough voting strength in the
United Nations, especially when the USSR and its allies vote with them,
frequently to carry the day even against the fierce opposition of the
USA, which has consequently withdrawn from such agencies as
UNESCO and, briefly, ILO.

The Third World has emerged with a new consciousness of itself –
reflected in the very term 'non-alignment', which identifies what holds
the countries together today, as opposed to the earlier geographical label
of the 'Afro-Asian' powers, which emphasized their common, colonial
past.

Yet the non-aligned identity is still a negative one, the voice of economic 'have-nots'. Their weakness is only too obvious. As a cynical

Asian diplomat long ago observed: 'Zero plus zero plus zero still equals zero.' Their increased numerical strength, too, is at the same time a drawback in that they constitute an assemblage of the most unlikely bedfellows: from Brunei, owned by the richest man in the world, to Cuba.

Few of them are prepared to follow Cuba's path and develop their economic ties with Communist countries. Such a policy invites, at best, economic isolation, even blockade; at worst, nuclear blackmail or the bombing 'back into the Stone Age' which Vietnam had to undergo, or the physical destruction inflicted on Nicaragua and Mozambique today. The weakness of the Soviet economy, already burdened to the tune of more than six billion dollars a year by the economic and military aid given to its allies, makes it impossible for the USSR to provide assistance to yet more states. The poor countries are therefore forced to compete, on hopelessly unequal terms and often with each other, for a marginal share of the world market.

There is, of course, a third possibility: expansion of South–South trade – a possibility now being explored by the non-aligned movement for the first time, following its last meeting in Harare. Julius Nyerere's visit to South America is an initial step.

Academic theories about the North–South divide – ranging from the school of dependency to the world-systems approach – have in general denied the possibility that the Third World can free itself from outside domination. The countries are seen as being trapped by neocolonial economic control or as being ensnared in an unmovable world system. More recent versions of these theories examine the new international division of labour, yet still omit agencies of resistance and radical change. World capitalism as a mode of production is today remarkably resilient, continually developing new forms across the globe. But Botswana is not Taiwan, and the whole of Black Africa is being left to rot.

In thinking about world inequality, most people resort to other models and explanations. Since very few people in the West actually visit the Third World, they inevitably derive their images of what life is like for the majority of humankind from old stereotypes and from the media, particularly television. And the greatest global event in the history of television, watched by more people than any other programme, was in fact an event focused on the Third World: the 1986 Live Aid rock concert sponsored by Bob Geldof in response to the disastrous drought in the Sahel zone of Africa, particularly in Ethiopia. The scale of the response to that appeal – and the support given, year in and year out, to the major Third World charities such as Oxfam and War on Want – reflects the profound concern of tens of millions of

people in the West, not about the successes of world capitalism but
about the miseries it creates.

No one would want for a minute to disparage that generosity. Yet
such is the scale of world poverty that it cannot possibly be seriously
mitigated by *ad hoc* disaster-triggered private responses, even on the
scale of Live Aid, or by the most energetic activity on the part of the
largest of the charities. Oxfam, for instance, has £32 million available for
overseas use: this would provide the 2,389,500,000 people in the thirty-
six poorest countries, from Ethiopia to Vietnam, with less than 14 pence
each. The four billion pounds handed over to the rich in Nigel Lawson's
1988 UK Budget is more than a thousand times as much as the income
which War on Want raises from the public to alleviate poverty among
three-quarters of humanity.

Racist and right-wing explanations of world poverty, especially in the
USA, blame the peoples of the Third World (they lack get-up-and-go)
or Third World elites, or assume that these countries are simply poorly
endowed by nature. They also usually conclude that the answers lie in
using more (Western) technology – what they need is know-how,
engineering, literacy – not in politics.

In the UK, the Thatcher years have resulted in a weakening of internationalism, an erosion that can be seen in the difference between the
popular response to Suez and public reaction to the Falklands War. It is
especially depressing that this apparent downturn in internationalism
results in the turning-down of the volume when the Labour Party speaks
about the Third World. It is not that Labour has a bad policy – the
policy document issued during the 1987 election campaign was probably
the best statement in this field that Labour has ever issued – but the
issue of development was conspicuously absent in the 1987 general election. As with nuclear disarmament, the opportunity to change and
create new policies which would grip the imagination of a new generation, which had been tapped by Bob Geldof, was deliberately thrown
away.

As Neil Kinnock rightly said after his crushing defeat, elections are
not won in a few months. New and radical policies have to be put across
in a sustained way, over a long period of time, and long-established
prejudices confronted, not just in the few weeks of an election
campaign. There is an obvious model for success immediately at hand:
Margaret Thatcher who, by preaching, day in and day out, the philosophy of the New Right, did not reflect public opinion, but changed it –
just what Marx told the left they should do.

As the New Left argued from the beginning, people in developed
nations can help to emancipate the majority of humankind from daily
poverty by building new non-exploitative relations with them. In recent

years, for example, some of the charity organizations have shifted towards a more radical economic and political view of the world system as the cause of poverty – blaming the multinationals, the banks and some Third World elites. Instead of relying on famine-relief campaigns, they emphasize policies of democratic self-help and economic development strategies based on 'appropriate' technology.

The drought in the Sahel, and the well-intentioned publicity of the charities, has unfortunately imprinted an indelible image of the Third World on the minds of most people in the West: the image of a skeletal black child with a begging bowl in his or her hands. But the people of the Third World are not simply impotent victims, people to whom things are done by more powerful Others. People in the Third World are constantly engaged, every day of their lives, in active response to the changes in their lives. Their responses are not usually revolutionary – the only ones to which people with barricade mentalities pay attention. Instead, there are the daily struggles of organizations like the Penang Consumer Association in Malaysia, which exposes the adulteration of basic foods and the marketing of dangerous goods, or the campaigns organized by the Kerala Sastra Sahithya Parishad in South India, in which thousands of health workers, teachers and scientists go to the villages and use traditional theatre as well as modern print to bring new ideas to millions of people. In Ahmedabad, outcaste women – mainly illiterate and confined to marginal employments men would not undertake, and debarred thereby from established trade unions – formed not only their own large and efficient union but even their own credit bank.

People today, from China to Latin America, are struggling for democratic rights, just as they struggled for independence when the New Left grew up. Then, national self-rule was the key issue for them and for us. Today, people in the Third World are struggling for genuinely autonomous trade unions; for the right to organize legal opposition parties; as exploited consumers. And the most exploited of all – women – are on the move everywhere. We should be working with all of them.

5

New Left Economic Policy

John Hughes

Although economics was not the primary focus of the New Left, economists made a number of important contributions. Among these were: a critique of the prevailing form of nationalization and a proposal for a comprehensive prices and incomes policy. *The Insiders*, published as a supplement to *Universities and Left Review* 3, revealed the network of private financial and industrial interests which dominated the nationalized industries in Britain. The New Left questioned the socialist nature of such a system and initiated a debate about alternative forms of social ownership. *A Socialist Wages Plan*, by Ken Alexander and John Hughes, marked a break from the traditional left-wing defence of free collective bargaining. It advocated instead a voluntary wage- and price-control policy as an essential component of a planned economy. Since then, the significance of such a policy as a means of progressively regulating inflation and growth has become apparent. John Hughes discusses both of these New Left economic initiatives and defends their contemporary relevance.

The New Left faced a situation that was quite similar to the one we face today. We were just as far into a period of Conservative rule. We were seeing then, as now, a total failure by the Labour Party, in its policy documents and election statements, to make any significant challenge to the 'new conservatism'. In those days everyone was telling us that we had to come to terms with working-class affluence, and those were the days when Macmillan actually managed the business cycles and the timing of general elections rather better than the Labour government did. All in all, we confronted many circumstances with which we must come to terms today.

But of course there were also differences, one of the main ones being that a mixed economy had just been created in Britain. Both ownership and, apparently, control were being shared between the public and private sectors. It was the first time we had had a substantial sector of nationalized industries working within the predominant capitalist framework. Under the Conservatives, there was the apparent continuity of this policy; what the Attlee government created continued under Conservative management. Most of the institutions of the welfare state and of public ownership saw very little change. Nationalization of the steel industry was the one contested area. I spent a great deal of time writing about it, initially in *The New Reasoner* and later for the Fabian Society.

The trouble was that Labour had not thought through what it wanted to do with the public sector, the nationalized industries and the mixed economy. The New Left started a crucially important debate about public ownership because not only was a critique of capitalism needed, but also a critique of public ownership. At the time, the Labour Party was not putting together a critique on either front. On the capitalism front it put out a document, called *Industry and Society*, that

97

asserted that big firms were serving the nation well. On the public-ownership front, its document *Public Enterprise* simply whitewashed what was happening in nationalized industry.

The differences between then and now come out most clearly when we look at the attitude of the present Conservative government to public ownership. The present government has dramatically changed the frontiers of ownership through different forms of privatization which we cannot begin to analyse here. At the same time, however, the Labour Party and the mainstream labour movement seem to have no effective way of criticizing or evaluating what the Conservatives actually are doing. Despite this, I am on the whole more hopeful about the socialist discussion of the late 1980s than I was about its predecessor thirty years ago. I am more hopeful because the transformation of the frontier, style and nature of public enterprise that Thatcherism has created, and the surrounding issues of public responsibility and control that arise, are inevitably putting socialist issues back on our agenda. We have to be grateful for Thatcherism: it has reinstated a very elaborate and important agenda about how, as a political community, we should handle monopoly power. What instruments are appropriate for controlling and regulating public and private enterprise? I now want to look at two of the debates initiated by the New Left which still have relevance today. The first concerns the criticisms which I and others in the New Left made of public ownership. The second concerns our proposal for a socialist wages plan.

Public Ownership and Nationalization

Thirty years ago there was a kind of blanketing and conforming sense that we had arrived. Apparently, we had actually achieved our goal; and apparently, our achievement was equally compatible with Conservative and Labour governments. At the end of the decade the Labour leader, Hugh Gaitskell, sought to capture this mood symbolically by striking Clause 4, the commitment to social ownership, out of the Labour Party's constitution. In fact, this was one moment when the New Left was actually able to have some kind of dialogue with a lot of the more traditional (if you like) 'state socialists' of the old brand, from the trade unions and elsewhere, who rose in defence of Clause 4. For example, I was asked by Michael Foot to write the Tribune pamphlet *Socialism for the Sixties.* (It actually sold a lot more copies than any New Left pamphlet I can remember!) There we were, actually fighting against Gaitskell, and on that symbolic issue we won, though we lost most of the others.

Against this background of complacency, the New Left tried to make people rethink the issues involved in creating a transition to socialism in Britain. As I have already suggested, we had to do two things. First, we had to analyse and criticize the nature of power and its organization in the world of capitalist enterprise and suggest some forms we could use to establish a credible control. Second – and more importantly at the time – we had to provide a critique of the public industries and the public sector and the way it was used.

Now a starting point for this critique was the issue of *Universities and Left Review* which carried a separately published supplement called *The Insiders*. This was a fairly elaborate piece of work: in particular, it set out the nature of the people who were managing all the nationalized industries and the other public organizations. What emerged was an extraordinary picture which showed the extent to which public-sector managers were interlocked with interest groups in the capitalist sector. Michael Barratt Brown did a tremendous piece of work in *ULR* mapping out what he called 'the controllers'. He showed the extraordinary network of power centred in the big financial companies operating in the private sector. These very same people were being brought together and were managing the public enterprises. That was the picture *The Insiders* portrayed, and it began to raise the question, in a very crude way, whether we should be thinking of replacing these people with some element – it asked for no more than an element – of workers' and consumers' representation. I think that *The Insiders* was intellectually impoverished, because all it did – as Labour, in a rather ineffectual top–downwards way, also did – was raise the issue of worker-directors on the boards of industries. It did not raise questions about the whole nature of the function of either public or private enterprise.

My contribution to this was, I think, slightly more persistent than the view offered by *The Insiders* because I argued in *ULR*, and also in a Fabian pamphlet, that the nationalized industries were an exploited sector in the first place. The total failure of socialists to think through how they wanted to handle the relationship between public and private enterprise meant that we had not thought through price policy. Instead, we got a policy of subsidizing capitalist industry by way of state-industry borrowings. The nationalized industries first toppled into massive and, in some cases, unmanageable indebtedness by selling cheap and then having to borrow, and consequently built up fixed indebtedness. But they also, of course, bought from the private sector, and when they bought from the private sector they bought from cartelized industries at cartel prices. So you had an internal process of exploitation on a vast scale. You must remember that we were a highly protected economy – all these order books went through into the British industries and the most shameless exploitation of public-sector investment programmes took place. Rather than replacing exploitation and profit by something that had a socialist character, the whole system was a degeneration of the price mechanism and profit-making that one saw operating anyway – it was a further degeneration of that process. And of course it subsequently continued in that way, with the Treasury becoming more and more shameless about it.

I argued that if you wanted to understand the nationalized industries, you did not have to analyse their organization – a great deal had already been written on that. Rather, you had to analyse their relationship to the private sector. As soon as you did that, you knew you had to change both the system and that relationship.

Later I went on to make what I think is a very significant point: the frontier that we erected around the nationalized industries in the 1940s was a critical mistake. We erected the frontier around those industries sensibly because we were creating a public monopoly power inside that frontier. What we were also doing, however, was preventing a nationalized industry from moving – as it might have done out of pure commercial logic – across that frontier and creating its own new enterprises, and thus extending the sector of public ownership. We had in reality offered Britain's cartelized industries the pledge that they would not witness competition from the public sector. So we locked the public industries inside their frontier, and that was an enormously damaging and dangerous thing to do.

Although reinforced by the policies of the Conservative governments in the 1950s, this was a continuity of policy from the 1945 Labour government. Despite its large parliamentary majority, when this government nationalized transport it put pages and pages of clauses in the crucial nationalization bill constraining the productive power of the transport undertakings that were coming into being. From the very beginning, we had this constraining frontier. That obviously locked in the monopoly power of the private sector as sellers, because the nationalized industries were not able to provide substitutes by taking the initiative and building up their own manufacturing subsidiaries, their own construction subsidiaries, or whatever.

The other point I want to make is that this kind of nationalization totally alienated people who worked in these enterprises because the main historical function of public ownership in this country had nothing to do with socialism at all. It had simply to do with the reorganization under a single management of the capital, equipment and technology of those industries so that they were using modern technology in an integrated way. This was done so that they could move to capital intensity and provide orderly delivery to the commercial sector of the infrastructure services that they needed. That meant that you actually displaced workers by the hundreds of thousands. When I talk to Ruskin College students about this, none of them has any idea of how many workers there were in the coal industry when it was nationalized. They just cannot believe, looking at the National Union of Mineworkers now with one hundred thousand members, that we were looking at a coal industry that had three-quarters of a million workers in employment.

What we found in coal, railways, and other areas – steel later on – was a displacement of workers not by the tens of thousands but by the hundreds of thousands. Naturally the interesting point, therefore, if you are trying to think about full employment, is that it was presumably up to the private sector to provide the jobs for workers displaced by this organization of the public sector. Someone else had to organize their employment. We never saw the deep contradictions in which we had enmeshed ourselves while trying to defend that sort of public ownership. It was our task in the New Left to start that big challenge, not in order to deride public ownership but precisely in order to look for a mode of organization and democratization that could be a challenge to the present system rather than a further form of exploitation and manipulation of the public base of capitalism. That is still, I think, a crucial issue.

A Socialist Wages Plan

The other issue I want to discuss is also important, but I shall be briefer. We were trying to think, in the New Left, of how one related the organized power of the unions to a socialist planned democratization and a redistribution of power and income. How could one use the trade unions and their strength in the factories to create a new momentum? It was the New Left, therefore – rather than, if you like, 'the right' – that began to talk about a wages plan. We called it 'a socialist wages plan', not an incomes policy. We did not put in the old slogan of the left which in the name of revolutionary politics limited the trade unions to free collective bargaining – it actually meant that you could make no major rearrangements within the system. That was where the Communist left stood. We were not taking their position. Nor were we taking the position which was common to the later stages of the Labour government of 1945 to 1951, and the Conservative government subsequently, of working on various forms of repressive incomes policy – either by doing quiet deals with the trade-union leaders, or by using differentially the power of the state to hold down pay demands in the public enterprises and public services, which was what the Conservatives were doing in the mid 1950s.

We were looking in between those two positions to the notion that one could galvanize people and generate a sense of movement, if we could create an *alliance* between some future Labour government and organized labour around a programme, dedicated both to redistributing income and to organizing in a more planned way the growth of the economy, and therefore of its real productive power and its base of real incomes. We wanted to achieve this in a balanced way so that you did not take the old, Stalinist technique of sacrificing current consumption in an enormous attempt to put investment into overdrive. We also wanted to operate in a way that consciously restrained inflation so that instead of having the unions scapegoated as the source of incomes pressure, we would be turning round and raising the crucial questions of how to control prices and monopoly profit, and how to bring a challenge to bear on the capitalist sector of industry. We were looking, in perhaps very limited and primitive ways, at how the elements of that conceptual framework could be put together. We still need to look at that today.

The notion of an alliance between the trade unions and Labour became critically important in the 1960s. We got it dramatically wrong, however, and Labour and the trade unions produced the wrong kinds of incomes policy and actually found themselves trapped back into short-term collective bargaining. When Labour was in office there was total abdication of major responsibilities to the Treasury in the name of incomes policy. This destroyed all the hope that was emerging from trade unions fighting for, and securing, long-term agreements and developing a more planned approach to collective bargaining in their own territories. Everyone was locked back into the box of short-term agreements and deference to the Treasury.

In the much more profound crisis of the 1970s, we saw a sort of incomes policy: the Social Contract. The rhetoric of the Social Contract was very close to what we were asking for in 1959 in *A Socialist Wages Plan*. But the Social Contract broke on the crucial question of whether the government was organizing its political and economic power to develop a balanced growth of the economy, or whether we were going to find ourselves retreating in the direction of Treasury wishes – that is, restrictive Treasury management of the financial and economic system and all that that implied.

In the mid 1970s we were still confronted with an unbalanced approach to an alliance between the trade unions and Labour. This approach had, certainly because of Jack Jones, elements of redistribution in it (such as a flat-rate pay norm and higher pensions for state pensioners) but the power barons never delivered in terms of industrial democracy or of a real wages policy, the underpinning of real wages, and the renewed growth of the system. So it broke. I do not think that meant that the New Left was wrong to raise this issue. We were right, and I think we continue to be right, because we still have to resolve these questions about how you organize any mass understanding of what it means to challenge the existing structure and distribution of income.

My experience in the 1970s was that a lot of the things we were beginning to talk about and argue for in the New Left – such as the possibility of selective pressure on industry to develop in ways that were desirable, or the possibility of powerful price controls – were all actually justified in practice. When it was seriously attempted by the Labour government, it worked very well. It was never brought into a coherent strategy because it would have changed the direction of politics, but I would say that a lot of the things we had been thinking about thirty years ago in a somewhat primitive way came through later. So we were not writing an agenda that is now obscure or obsolete, and examining the New Left today should not be thought of as only an exercise in nostalgia. We were trying to tease out the way in which one could break the deadlock of a capitalist-controlled economy which was failing to develop to meet the needs of all the people and was locked into a very sterile approach to the use of power, at a time when the Labour Party appeared not to be offering a challenge. I do think that today, as compared to back then, we are in a much more dangerous situation. Today we are closer to the erosion of democracy and to a drift towards totalitarianism than we were thirty years ago. We have a weaker and more unbalanced economy than we had in 1957. So we now face a much more urgent task, but I still think that the agenda written by the New Left remains progressive.

6

Women in the New Left

During one of the conference sessions, Jean McCrindle (former co-ordinator of the Scottish New Left Clubs) observed that 'there was an almost pathological absence of women both in the content of the journals and of women who were writing', and that women 'felt almost totally silenced during that period'. These comments proved provocative enough to determine the content of the ensuing discussion and also to prompt us, in collecting material for this book, to ask women who were active in the early New Left to write about their experiences.

Sheila Benson recounts her increasingly active and outspoken, but in certain respects still silent, involvement in the London New Left Club. Dorothy Wedderburn, in extracts from an interview conducted in April 1988, adds her recollections as a former member of the Communist Party who was engaged during that period mainly in CND and Labour Party campaigns. Lynne Segal's elaboration of her response to Jean McCrindle at the conference is based on her own research on the 'Angry Young Men' of the 1950s. She argues that the silence of women up to the late 1960s is not surprising given the social, cultural and political context of post-war Britain.

These three pieces represent to us only the beginnings of a much-needed inquiry into the history of women in the 1950s and 1960s, and more specifically the history of women in the New Left. As more women contribute to the discussion of the still problematic role of women in left theory and activism, we hope that their suggestions for change will result in the creation of a real space for women on the left.

Experiences in the London New Left

Sheila Benson

Accounts of recent history by the participants themselves are likely to be somewhat disorderly: memory may be fitful and the experience was personal as well as political, part of being young and making friends within a new kind of socialist project.

The women I came to know in the New Left were predominantly from a graduate or professionally qualified or middle-class background. I was none of these things: my origin was working-class. Although I had stayed on in the sixth form and left school with useful pieces of paper that much later allowed me to enter full-time university education, I had no such ambitions at the time: I earned my living as an invoice typist. A member of the Communist Party until about the end of 1958, I had spent 1955–56 working in East Berlin for the Women's International Democratic Federation, which comprised many nationalities and was concerned with issues ranging from basic mother-and-child health care in less developed nations to women and trade unionism in the USA and Western Europe.

By 1957 I was what was then called an 'unmarried mother'. Full-time work and childcare responsibilities meant limited free time. But constraints on time and energy were secondary to the financial constraints of low pay: my take-home pay in those pre-decimal days was around £8 to £9 weekly, so that even tube fares to evening events played havoc with my budget, and participation in the early days of the New Left would have been ruled out had payments for babysitting to be found. When I became the second secretary of the London New Left Club, a gay male friend and work colleague insisted he would babysit on any evening when meetings, events or administrative concerns required my presence at the Club office in Carlisle Street.

Although the role of a secretary may carry gender-stereotyped over-tones, in the London New Left Club it did not include making tea or taking tickets at the door of public meetings (a responsibility of the male treasurer). It did include full membership of the executive committee. Moreover, secretarial tasks were often shared out within a general atmosphere of spontaneity and co-operation rather than any rigid division of labour.

I had never before spoken in any political forum. I still vividly recall how my first short contribution to an executive committee meeting of the New Left Club, which was taken up and seriously examined, was an important breakthrough towards a gain in confidence. When I was subsequently asked to chair or speak at public meetings, I was filled with nameless terror on each occasion. The intellectual and oratorical strengths of a number of male comrades were impressive but also intimidating. But the personal manner in which most men and women worked together, combined with occasional social opportunities to meet comrades who were also becoming friends, allowed me to begin to enter the spaces that were there to be occupied and to arrive at a small but important increase in experience. Any advance towards political confidence for women in the late 1950s and early 1960s, however halting and modest, helped to lay the foundations for a later and qualitatively different raising of consciousness.

While I want to record this positive aspect of one woman's experience in the New Left, I should add that the struggle to extend confidence, which was encouraged by most of the male comrades I saw frequently, could be set back by just one insensitive remark. After I had introduced a session on the clubs at a New Left weekend conference, for instance, a man commented (words engraved on my heart): 'That was a pretty *bizarre* offering'. I fled to the railway station. My reaction was to blame *myself* and disappear into a spiral of self-deprecation. Yet he had not had the slightest intention of putting me down: he simply lacked understanding of my anxiety as a speaker on public platforms.

Although I find it difficult to speak for other women comrades in the New Left – particularly without having had time for research – Jean McCrindle's reference, at the 1987 Oxford Conference, to the silence and the 'almost pathological absence of women both in the content of the journals and of women who were writing' prompted me to reflect on the extent to which women participated in the London Club activities. It seems to me that the ranks of activists were made up more or less equally of women and men. There was an extensive network of women which was partly established through the existence of the London Club. The shared experience of women included much time and energy spent on the tedious administrative and organizational chores, but a number of the men voluntarily undertook or shared such tasks.

In the large *public* meetings, women were silent/silenced. The invited speakers and those from the audience who contributed to discussion were overwhelmingly male. It was not that women were less interested in, or lacked an informed perspective on, the topics addressed at packed and usually compelling meetings. Had we raised our hands to speak, we would not have been invisible to the man in the chair. But for women, I suspect, the sheer size of the gatherings may have been daunting. Male comrades competed to say their piece in such numbers that the chair had difficulty in fitting in all those who indicated a readiness to speak before the rent on the hall ran out. Also, some male socialists were accustomed to a style of haranguing speaker and audience that sits uncomfortably with many women. So we reserved discussion of issues for smaller, informal groups.

The New Left did not prefigure the women's movement. Although some of us were to join it, our generation was not the main force behind its rise. Whilst we were alive to racial discrimination, to Notting Hill and apartheid, we were only faintly tuned in to sexual discrimination, focusing on 'double standards' and sexuality rather than structures of discrimination. Thus I have no recollection of women themselves calling into question the absence of their voices from the large public meetings. Looking back, I am interested that we were *collectively* inhibited, despite the fact that our ranks contained a high proportion of remarkable women whose contributions in their fields of employment gained recognition and esteem.

Why were women not on the agenda? Perhaps Robin Blackburn, at the Oxford Conference, picked out one strand when he suggested that Simone de Beauvoir's *Second Sex* 'had a rather delayed time-bomb effect . . . for some reason it raised issues for people privately but not publicly'. Before I got around to de Beauvoir, I read Doris Lessing's *The Golden Notebook*. The impact of either book on a receptive woman reader then would indeed have been subject to a time-delay: for the deeply personal was not only being *published*, but *politicized*. *The Golden Notebook* was the first book I had read that suggested that many of the 'problems' I was conditioned to think of as my own, to contend with as best I could, were in fact part of the experience of other women. I was unable fully to discuss the implications of the book until I had confronted them myself.

Second, if women were not on the agenda, culture was: the analysis of culture was a crucial part of the work of the New Left. Yet there are ways in which a concern with culture may marginalize or even obscure *structural* oppression. Because the immensely important project of developing the analysis of culture was undertaken by male socialists of the New Left, the focus was on male culture. As a consequence, women were marginalized in this analysis.

A third strand of explanation – probably the most important – relates to the context of the period and, more specifically, the gains for women in post-war welfare provision. The young women of the New Left generation were experiencing those gains. Women and their children now had their own right of access to a national health service and to social security. I could be both a single parent and a full-time employee because some local authorities maintained day nurseries. Other women were benefiting from increased access to higher education and the steady expansion of professional occupations. Even women following the same kind of manual or semi-skilled occupations as their mothers – the vast majority, then as now, of women in paid employment – were about to experience 'the consumer revolution' and its new labour-saving domestic appliances, hire purchase, changes in retail distribution and package holidays. At the same time we all continued to respond to certain kinds of traditional stimuli important to capitalist ideology and profit – like, for instance, fashion: many of us wobbled on stiletto heels or crammed our feet into winkle-pickers and later adopted the miniskirt.

If, in retrospect, the New Left has to be regarded as gender-blind, I nevertheless consider it unhistorical to blame the men of the New Left for failing to understand that the women of the New Left lived and worked within a patriarchal structure of power. We were all prisoners of history, and the women themselves were unaware of the need to challenge the assumption that women had achieved equality with men in the post-war welfare state.

Many of us stopped short for a decade or more before beginning to recognize our oppression. At the time, I existed in a state of false consciousness about my position as a woman – and this was also the case for some of the women I knew best – although I would have denied it hotly had it been put to me. For I was involved with political questions I took as urgent and compelling and was working with like-minded comrades, who also offered new and stimulating ideas.

Most importantly, the New Left seemed to be making a contribution towards breaking the fetters of Stalinist and Fabian monopolies on socialist analysis and discussion. As such it was hospitable to a heterogeneous collection of casualties from the Suez and Hungary débâcles: women and men from this and other countries, members of minority groupings. If the New Left is judged by the present generation of young socialists to have been wanting in its response to women, it still contrasts favourably with the trade-union movement and the Labour and Communist Parties of that period. The lack of hospitality of those political arenas – a combination of the bureaucratic structure of meetings, formal discourse and predominance of male voices – may have helped to account, in part, for the influx of women into the New Left.

Activism and the New Left*

Dorothy Wedderburn

I stayed in the Communist Party (CP) because most people in the Cambridge branch were critical for the same sort of reasons that I was, wanting to review a whole lot of fundamental issues, and we were able to do that together for a time. Almost as soon as I had left the CP I joined the Labour Party. Again, in Cambridge, it was a very sympathetic local Labour Party. We had in fact a very good left-wing Labour candidate who was for nuclear disarmament and all these sorts of things. So it was a natural home in which to be politically active at the local level.

I never participated in a New Left group as such. I knew about the New Left Club in London, and I knew people in it, but by that time I had become very involved with the nuclear disarmament movement, when it was still not very popular on the left. We started a group in Cambridge which antedated what became a small national movement against Britain testing its own nuclear weapons. That was my main focus of political activity from then on right the way through.

What I found appealing about the New Left was the opening up of questions. My reasons for leaving the CP did not have to do just with the horror of Hungary or the shattering of illusions about the Soviet Union, but also with the increasing dissatisfaction with the CP's policy in this country and the fundamental questioning about how we could produce social change, and so on. So the New Left, to the extent that it was opening up those sorts of questions, was very attractive.

But I wasn't attracted by what I regarded at times as the very great emphasis on theorizing and less on direct political action. I suppose the form that the theoretical discussion took did not particularly appeal to me. I was always very much concerned with the politics of getting people

*Extracts from an interview

111

elected or getting policies adopted and general grass-roots political activity. I did a lot of speaking at that time for CND and its predecessors, and that took precedence over the theoretical approaches.

I don't think there was ever any deliberate exclusion of women – of course, these things are usually not deliberate: there was no attempt to exclude women. Maybe women were more diffident. Of course, one forgets how much more sensitive one is now, and it's quite hard, unless you spend a lot of time thinking about it, to reconstruct what was actually going on and how much of the assumed roles were being allocated.

I never felt that I, or women I knew, were given the organizational tasks to do, or were not expected to speak. But that is probably due to our Communist Party background, because the one thing that has been invaluable for people who were in the CP for any length of time was the kind of training you got. It was your responsibility to speak out in non-Communist Party gatherings, so you simply learned to force yourself to contribute to discussions in a way which didn't discriminate between the sexes; and that just carried over. But that is very much an aspect of intellectual, academic Communists: it was always a problem in working-class CP branches to get the women involved and to get the men to see them involved in an equal way. The attitude of working-class men to women's participation was very often discussed in the CP, but it was taken for granted that one was equal in the academic milieu.

So the question of women's involvement is something that didn't occur to me in relation to my own role, or in relation to the activities in which I primarily engaged. But it certainly raised its head in relation to the Labour Party, where a traditional branch activity would be women doing the bazaars and the money-raising, and maybe by and large not the speaking – although you'd certainly have to put exceptions to that, of course. Again this was seen by people like me and my contemporaries as a problem – but not for us, as it were. It was a problem because of attitudes which were not held among intellectuals. So I was a bit surprised that it was so apparent to people like Jean McCrindle, after the event: that she saw this relegation of women.

Also I don't think there was a feeling that certain things were 'women's concerns' in the milieu in which I was moving in Cambridge at that time. That's illustrated by the amount of public speaking we did, although not necessarily at a national level. But, for example, in CND I spoke at a lot of public meetings in East Anglia; also for the Labour Party, I would talk about economic policy – and I don't think that's particularly a 'women's thing'. In CND there was sometimes a bit of a labelling because, particularly on nuclear testing, there was a big campaign about the dangers of fallout; and so there were particular meetings for women. And I think I'm right in saying that probably the speakers would all have been chosen as women then. That was perhaps appealing to the audience.

Thinking about how few women were contributing to the New Left journals, I was struck by the fact that in so far as the women writing for the journals were in fact all academics, and at that time the proportion of women going to university was much lower than it is today, the low number of women contributors was reflecting the sex structure in the universities. This may help, in part, to explain it. There was no issue of principle involved in the fact that I did not write for *Universities and Left Review* or *New Left Review* – that I was asked and refused, or anything like that. But what I was writing and thinking about – and this also applies to my contribution to the *May Day Manifesto* – was very much linked with my own interests and research in poverty, inequality and social policy, and my memory is that these journals didn't carry an awful lot on those subjects: they had much more theoretical interests.

The Silence of Women in the New Left*

Lynne Segal

Looking back today, Jean McCrindle commented, women's silence seems quite incredible, almost pathological. But if we look at the experiences and assumptions surrounding women's (and men's) lives at the time, the silence is not so surprising.

The first clue to this 'pathological' silence of, and about, women in those days is that the left in the fifties was as silent as everyone else on relations between the sexes because it accepted unquestioningly a belief central to the fifties consensus: women's problems had been solved. In fact, the myth that women's problems were a thing of the past, that the sexes were now equal, was as central to the post-war consensus as the supposed disappearance of class antagonism.

The second clue is the force of the assumed biological imperative of motherhood and childcare which emerged more strongly in the fifties than it ever had before. Every social problem, the psychological wisdom of the time insisted, could be attributed to inadequate mothering. The prevalent assumption then was that if women with children had jobs, it was because they were 'forced to' through poverty. Mothers would not choose to work. Woman's place was so absolutely in the home that women were no more able than men at the time to question domestic arrangements and to suggest any alternative solutions to the strains placed upon women isolated in the home or, increasingly, going out to work but expected to give complete priority to their families. What was needed was a whole new way of thinking about marriage, child-rearing, sexuality and employment, and that just wasn't available either to women or to men at the time.

---

*The themes and ideas expressed in this article are further developed in: L. Segal, 'Look Back in Anger: Men in the Fifties', in *Male Order*, ed. Rowena Chapman & Jonathan Rutherford, London 1988.

A third point is that although in the fifties the woman's place was in the home, the consensus at the time assumed that women could hardly have cause to complain of this – for now the man's place was also in the home. Men too, in popular consciousness, were being domesticated, had returned from battlefield to bungalow with new expectations of the comforts and pleasures of home. Almost all the writing of the fifties celebrates a new *togetherness*, harmony, and equality between women and men in the home. But the man-about-the-house still occupied a separate sphere from women – even in the home. He did the gardening and all manner of do-it-yourself hobbies: he didn't change the nappies, do the housework; this was not his job. Again expert opinion suggested that the man-in-an-apron could cause psychological damage to his sons by supplying an inadequate sex-role model.

Fourthly, it does seem to be true that the image of the domesticated male did create a lot of tension and, as some were to describe it, 'crisis' over 'manhood' in the fifties. This was particularly acute because of the post-war contrast between wartime and civilian life, perpetuated until the early sixties through the maintenance of universal military conscription marking men's entry into adulthood. Certainly the bravado and male bonding of conscript life strengthened what were in fact the prevalent tensions and conflicts between men and women in the fifties. No amount of celebrated 'togetherness' between the sexes could really hide the fact that the fifties, still without abortion or contraception rights for women, was a time of enormous mistrust and hostility between women and men. Woman-hating, homophobia and men's fear of their own 'weakness' or 'femininity' constituted the hallmark of fifties masculinity. The ongoing dismantling of the 'British Empire' and the Cold War climate both exacerbated national anxieties over manhood and fears of national weakness and decline at the time. A sex war, and hysterical persecution of gay people, accompanied the Cold War.

Finally, taking us right into the heart of the New Left and the silence of and about women at the time, was the impact of the so-called 'Angry Young Man' on radical culture and politics in the fifties. Women and domesticity were seen as the archenemy of the freedom-loving anarchic young working-class rebel of the day. Men of the New Left identified strongly with the tough, amoral, cynical, invariably misogynist heroes of Allan Sillitoe, John Osborne and others. Women were never to be trusted but treated as part of the system trying to trap, tame and emasculate men. A stifling domesticity had killed the spirit and guts of men, these 'rebels' declared, and women were to blame. What was really happening in most of the 'Angry' literature was that class hostility was suppressed and twisted into new forms of sexual hostility.

Amidst all this taunting and blaming of women, amidst the general blindness – of men and women alike – to any issues of gender or problems of women, it seems to me not very surprising that so few women were writing or speaking publicly and prominently at the time. The wonder is more that in ten short years we were to become so confidently vociferous. Things really did change – but that is another story.

7

The New Left as a Social Movement

Michael Rustin

The intellectual and cultural vitality of the New Left contrasts starkly with its relative political weakness. While the New Left clubs enjoyed large memberships and were lively centres of debate in many towns and cities throughout Britain, the movement's ideas failed to gain a permanent foothold in the labour movement or in the established political parties. Michael Rustin argues that this failure can be explained by the nature of the New Left as a social movement. He suggests that it was initiated by – and appealed primarily to – members of an 'expanded class of cultural and intellectual workers'. The New Left's political weakness, he argues, resulted from its inability to find political roots outside this limited social base and to build alliances with the traditional labour movement and other constituencies of the left.

Thinking about the significance of the New Left in Britain, one is struck above all by the contrast between its great cultural and intellectual vitality, whose effects are still strongly evident today, and its much more limited and disappointing political impact. I mean not only that since the mid 1970s we have been enduring a sustained period of political reaction, but that even within the Labour Party and working-class and radical movements more generally, the New Left has been at best an intermittent and minority presence. However, the recent success of the New Right and the earlier political failure of the New Left are probably connected. Had the Labour Party absorbed more in the 1960s of the concerns and practices of the New Left, its governments would have been more able to manage the new social tensions which beset them, and less powerless to comprehend their own plight in intellectual terms. In fact, some of the relevant lessons have been better learned by the New Right than by Labour – for example: how to mobilize opinion against entrenched institutions; how to generate and use ideas in political ways; even how, occasionally, to link mass protests with parliamentary struggles. Thatcherism has demonstrated in a curious way that it is possible to succeed politically by going against the grain of the Establishment, and by mobilizing social forces which feel partially excluded and ignored by large institutions.

The intellectual and cultural fertility of the New Left was recognized early on even by its opponents. The love-hate relationship of *Universities and Left Review* with Anthony Crosland was reciprocated. The early New Left and the 'modernizers' of the Labour right shared the conviction that there needed to be a debate about the changing shape of this society, and that Labour could not live by its traditional formulae alone. Some liberals had a fantasy of detaching the younger revisionist elements of the New Left, with their attractive new agenda of issues, from their much less welcome Marxist attachments. As it became clear to all that this movement retained its integral links with the Marxist tradition, even though it was very critical of its orthodoxies, the warmth shown at times by liberals towards *ULR* and the work of Raymond Williams soon faded.

How can we account for this discrepancy between cultural vitality and political weakness? What happened to this 'movement', both of ideas and of people, as it liked to describe itself? The idea of the New Left as a 'movement' was always a vision and an aspiration more than it was a substantial reality. The concept 'movement' was adopted in order to differentiate this new political practice from that of conventional bureaucratic political parties, whether of the orthodox Communist or Labour varieties. The idea was that a movement was fluid, open, participatory and inclusive, closely in touch with living communities in ways which parties had mostly ceased to be.

The Campaign for Nuclear Disarmament was the first practical model for this, and its size and innovative qualities (reinventing, so to speak, the mass march, the political anthem, civil disobedience, political symbols and banners) for a few years made the idea of a mass movement of the New Left seem feasible. Later, the civil-rights movement in the United States, the mass mobilizations in response to the Vietnam War, the more general uprisings of the late 1960s, and the women's liberation movement showed how prescient this counterposing of 'movement politics' to conventional party politics had been.

Eventually the idea of 'new social movements' in contradiction to party and class institutions became part of formal political theory, years after these innovations were explored in practice. It has often been difficult to tell whether the New Left's innovations in theory and practice (community organizing in Notting Hill, debates on workers' control, the agendas of cultural politics, and so on) were merely the first swallows of a summer that was in any case bound to come or whether they really had a significant influence on later developments – no doubt sometimes one, sometimes the other.

But while the first New Left certainly sought to relate itself to these various new movements, one after another as they emerged, its own specific attempts to establish itself as a political formation on the ground encountered difficulties. It is true that in its early days *New Left Review* could proudly proclaim the existence of forty-odd left clubs up and down the country. In London, the *ULR* Club and later the New Left Club had an amazing success in attracting weekly audiences of hundreds of people to meetings on an enormous range of subjects. Suddenly, the political agenda was completely redefined and opened up. Literature (especially that of commitment), history (especially that of the 1930s and of communism), art and architecture, social theory, youth culture, class, neutralism and the Cold War, and the more 'conventional' political issues of poverty, social policy, economic planning and education, succeeded one another as the week's topic.

Speakers were drawn from an equally unexpected range. The New Left editors themselves (from both *ULR* and *The New Reasoner* branches), survivors of the thirties like Wal Hannington, veterans of the European revolutions like Isaac Deutscher, close comrades from the parallel New Left movements in Europe like Claude Bourdet, writers, artists and architects – even Labour politicians were invited to speak. This was simultaneously a renaissance of the political tradition of the Popular Front which had been buried during the Cold War, and the birth of a new generation of radical socialists brought together in lively and sometimes moving synthesis. For someone in the sixth form of a suburban grammar school, as I was at the time, it was an incredible experience to be exposed to this ferment of ideas, covering just about everything in which an eighteen-year-old could conceivably be interested. These meetings, and the commitments and friendships to which they gave rise, had a lifelong effect on many people who took part in them.

Nevertheless, this was not quite the substance of a political movement. It was, as Edward Thompson frequently pointed out, the metropolis, and it was easy to mistake the interest that new ideas could arouse among the meeting-goers of a capital city for rooted political involvement. The founding of a left-wing coffee bar in Soho (the Partisan) suggests the desire of the New Left to make a congenial home for itself in the capital city, rather than a determination to win over its citizens. Outside London left club activities mostly took place on a smaller scale, though they were often more closely connected to the mainstream political life of the left in these towns than similar activities in central London.

Often the function of the clubs was to bring together thoughtful activists from different fragments and organizations – the Communist Party, the Labour Party, International Socialists, CND and non-aligned socialists – who normally found little occasion to meet. Even so, around half the clubs were in university towns and depended to a considerable degree on the interest generated by the journal, and on the committed efforts of its editors at this time to sustain them.

There was always a tension between the priority to be given to the journal and the work of the clubs. This sometimes appeared in the form of resentment, by spokespersons for the North, of the irrelevant preoccupations of the capital. Actually, the cultural power concentrated in Britain by a nexus based on London–Oxford–Cambridge is a general problem, not peculiar to the experience of the New Left. When a new editorial board of *NLR* revealed its indifference to the left clubs they rapidly dwindled, even though many of their members remained central to the life of the left in their various cities. But it was clear that the clubs were far from being an autonomous or self-sustaining political force. Only CND's strength, and the New Left's influential relationship with it, made the New Left's view of itself as a movement seem plausible. CND was not, however, the New Left.

In some universities, where *ULR* had begun, it was possible, for a few years in the late 1950s and 1960s, to reproduce an intensity of excitement and commitment similar to that which was seen in the London New Left Club. The New Left, closely allied with CND, became in Oxford one side of the main political debate in the university. It was possible to work effectively within the mainstream political clubs, maintaining reasonable debate with the Labour right. At one stage there was a Labour Club membership of around a thousand, very big meetings, and a range of speakers which, as in London, extended from the normal routine of front-bench Labour politicians to New Left intellectuals, writers and academics. There were magazines founded, like *New University* in Oxford, following in their own way the example of *NLR* and exerting some wider influence on university journalism. This was not altogether unimportant, since it was the creation of the intensity of interest which enabled the New Left to recruit new participants from one generation to the next. It is wrong to see the first New Left as something which merely existed between 1956 and 1962. There are many threads of continuity, and many individuals, who link up one phase with the next, responding to changing situations and moods, but nevertheless bearing the initial impulses forward. The development and reproduction of an enlarged radical culture was one of the major achievements of that process.

Why, however, did all this political energy and inventiveness fail to lead to the formation of any organized or solid political force, either as a major fraction of the Labour Party or as an independent party of the left? Neither in this first phase nor in several subsequent attempts over twenty years (the *May Day Manifesto*, *Beyond the Fragments*, the Socialist Society) has it proved possible to maintain a territorially organized base for political activity for more than a year or two, and never on a genuinely national scale.

The central reason for this is that the New Left was closely linked to a very specific social development, of which it was only partially aware. This was the emergence of an enlarged class of intellectual and cultural workers, in late capitalist society in Britain and elsewhere. In the period from 1960 to 1980 the numbers of students in higher education in

Britain nearly trebled: from under 200,000 full-time students to nearly 600,000. The occupational structure also radically altered, with the rise of a new service class of professionals, teachers, planners and administrative workers, many of them drawn into the rapidly expanding public sector. Alongside these new or enlarged occupations, and the educational systems which supplied them, a cultural infrastructure of publishing, journalism and arts activities developed. People who felt that people of their kind and background had never had access or public means of expression before were brought into the cultural system.

To a great extent the New Left represented new voices making themselves heard in the complacent climate of British middle-class culture: working-class voices, through drama, film (both actors and directors), in fiction and in the critical, theoretical and autobiographical writings of Raymond Williams, Richard Hoggart, and soon many others. And new generational voices – a cult of youth suffused the left in this period as well as soon dominating the media and popular culture generally. British class culture was so pervasive and restrictive that many educated in grammar or art schools, coming from lower-middle-class families or even families established in business or professional occupations, felt sharply antagonistic to the dominant elite and its status-ridden assumptions. It turned out that many of the oppositional radicals of that time – most of those around *Private Eye*, for example, or writers like John Osborne or Kingsley Amis – were not really on the left at all. They did not share its collective loyalties and sentiments but were intransigent individualists, hostile and competitive towards what was then called 'the Establishment'. Nevertheless the range of oppositional voices was still important in establishing a mood in which the New Left could take up a significant place.

In this climate, voices suppressed or marginalized in the recent period resurfaced – hence intellectual work in the British Marxist tradition could resume a vigorous development. The social and generational forces which underlay the emergence of new radicalism in Britain also gave rise to the Kennedy phenomenon in the United States. Both were founded on a cult of youth and education. The sense of betrayed idealism of that American moment then led to the intensity and fury of the political battles of the late 1960s.

Some of the 'voices' which have been crucial to the later development of the left, in the 1970s and 1980s, were only barely audible in the early stage. This is true of black consciousness (though the importance of West Indian writing and culture was recognized from the first); of the presence of a distinctive gay culture and identity, just traceable in the creative output of the early New Left (for example, in Shelagh Delaney's play *A Taste of Honey*); and also to a considerable extent of feminism, despite the presence of Doris Lessing (a member of *The New Reasoner*'s editorial board) and the influence she came to have through her fiction. This mainly reflects the somewhat later rise in the number and proportion of women in post-sixteen and post-school education, especially outside the traditional female preserve of teacher training. It was the experience of this generation of women graduates, who left the relatively free setting of college and found themselves again subjected to the (male-dominated) pressures of family and workplace, which gave feminist politics its critical mass in terms of numbers and shared experience.

In Oxford and Cambridge in those days – to cite the locations from which most of the founding group had come – the proportion of male to female undergraduates was 10 to 1. The dominant attitudes to gender relations were an uneasy combination of gentlemanly indulgence and puritanical repression, neither at all enlightened. It seems to me that to berate the New Left of those early days for its sexism is to rely excessively on hindsight. Most people in this situation, of both sexes, felt themselves to be victims and the pain and anger of the situation, especially for women, still remained for the most part to be publicly articulated. I doubt if this climate of gender relations could have been effectively challenged sooner than it was.

The New Left was successful, for some years, as a multidimensional expression of these emergent presences in British culture. Its strength was that it sought to unify, in a common project, a great diversity of experiences and issues, without seeking to reduce them to formulae or subject them to organizational discipline. A visible but creative minority culture of the left emerged in most of the arts and also in most branches of academic activity, post-school education being one of the main growth areas. The New Left succeeded, so to speak, by cultural sector in a way that it never did or could have done in terms of territory. This is because its crucial constituencies were strongly concentrated in certain professional occupations – teaching, social work, architecture, acting, journalism, film-making, even science – but by the nature of things were thinly scattered over the country as a whole. Movements of intellectuals unavoidably have a peculiar geographical distribution. (For this reason the Left Bank had a seductive attraction for some in the New Left even before 1968.)

When *ULR* and *The New Reasoner* were started, these two precarious journals represented almost the whole of serious left journalism except for the traditional party journals, Fabian pamphlets, and the *New Statesman.* Later, each sector of radical intellectual activity came to have its own journal, its own conference, and its own specific public – *Critical Social Policy, Radical Philosophy, Radical Science Journal,*

History Workshop, the Conference of Socialist Economists and its journal *Capital and Class*, and many others. There is a vast growth over this period of networks and resources able to articulate oppositional meaning and political definition. This, and the related equally important changes which have taken place in the arts, have altered the whole quality of what it is like to feel part of the left, at least in a large city in Britain. The available cultural menu now allows people to live their whole lives in a radical intellectual culture in a way that one could not easily do in the 1950s. This has certainly been a success of a kind, though in terms much narrower than were hoped for in the populist and outward-looking vision of the early days. This partial success may also, as Raphael Samuel has pointed out, have its own costs in the self-isolation of the left. Compared with the relative security of life within a subculture, where most values are held in common, the task of making socialism appealing to the majority may come to seem both difficult and threatening.

1968 saw a major break in the left's culture and political style – bringing to it a new intensity and intransigence. This has various explanations, not least a general heightening of class and other antagonisms as the balance of social forces shifted for some years in favour of working-class and other subordinate groups. The sheer numbers exposed to radical culture, in the universities and elsewhere, created a new critical mass, whereas the previous generation had been more conscious of its relative isolation and marginality, and perhaps more hopeful that changes might be won from the system by force of persuasion. But although there was a notable change in climate – and later a determined counter-reaction by the right – the social dynamics of this second-stage New Left, and especially its predominant base in the new intelligentsia, had an essential continuity with the first.

The theoretical work which underpinned the early New Left also reflected its particular social base. Culture and meaning were always the dimensions most central to its vision of the world. This was a preoccupation which derived from the New Left's own dependence – as its 'economic base', so to speak – on newly acquired cultural capital. Historically, this was projected backwards in an identification with earlier generations of political and cultural critics, for whom extended literacy had also been a crucial resource. The central idea of Raymond Williams's *The Long Revolution* was that of a learning community, the idea of a people who in the long term gain access to the cultural powers of meaning-generation. The idea of cultural empowerment was a key addition by Williams to the dominant British socialist conception (articulated most clearly in T.H. Marshall's essay 'Citizenship and Social Class') of an evolution of civil, political, and social rights. (This idea has not been well taken by the Labour Party.)

Edward Thompson's argument in *The Making of the English Working Class* and elsewhere was more combative in tone, but nevertheless shared some of these basic assumptions. Here too the central image was of working people creating a new class identity through the power of language and speech, and with the help of the voices and pens of exemplary populist intellectuals like William Cobbett and William Morris (figures whose courageous role Thompson himself has followed in many admirable respects). Stuart Hall's work, likewise, has been to establish the importance of cultural definition, both in the terms of directly political discourses, developing Gramsci's ideas, and in relation to broader kinds of cultural and subcultural expression. Two institutions or networks founded by members of this founding generation – the Centre for Contemporary Cultural Studies, and History Workshop and its publications – have had major roles in the redefinition of cultural production: who makes culture, and where.

This centrality of culture to the New Left, I contend, has not been merely a weakness or an academic diversion from 'real political work'. (Incidentally, a similar emphasis is to be found in the work of leading intellectuals to the left elsewhere in Europe – for example, that of Habermas, Bourdieu, or Foucault.) It reflects the enhanced importance of cultural work and cultural workers in a society in which the service, information and people-processing industries, and the new occupations they generate, have become central. As a rising class fraction in the 1960s, these groupings were radical and optimistic in their sentiments and aspirations. Thus the New Left found some real resonance and social roots.

Its relation, however, to the wider constituencies of the left, especially the labour movement, was always more difficult. The greater ease of work with CND was mainly due to the fact that CND's active support was largely drawn from occupational groups – teachers, social workers, and so on – similar to those of the New Left itself. The conventional relation of Labour intellectuals, including some politicians, to the labour movement then implied too much latent deference and patronage to be comfortable for the New Leftists. Nor, on the other hand, was a more militantly labourist identity really consistent with the New Left's self-identification. The most organic link with the labour movement was characteristically effected through the channel of workers' education – through trade-union colleges, research departments, and links with a few significant trade-union leaders, such as Lawrence Daly of the National Union of Mineworkers. It was no coincidence that the two individuals who were most significant in the early New Left's trade-union educational and research work, Michael Barratt Brown and John Hughes, later became principals respectively of Northern College and Ruskin, the two trade-union colleges.

A similar pattern of influence was seen in the work of the Institute of Workers' Control (IWC) during the 1970s. Its leading figures, Ken Coates and Tony Topham, also worked in adult education. The IWC did win considerable influence in the Labour Party during the 1960s for a programme of industrial democracy, culminating in the publication of the ill-fated Bullock Report in 1977 (though not support enough to win over a majority of unions to what would have amounted to a large change in the trade unions' role). Thus, despite energetic efforts in the late 1950s and early 1960s (including a vivid journalistic presence at Labour Party conferences via a witty daily news commentary distributed to delegates), the first New Left had only a limited impact on the Labour Party, either through individuals or ideas. The more sectarian formations of the 1970s and early 1980s turned out to be better adapted to capturing real power in the Party than the more diffuse and intellectually orientated New Left intelligentsia. 'One foot in and one foot out' was never going to be a strong position to push from, and the revealing physical absurdity of this image never seemed to be noticed at the time.

It was only when the new municipal authorities came into office later on – especially in London, where the weight of the traditional working class was less than elsewhere – that the later generation of the New Left found a firm base inside major Labour Party institutions. This was owed in part to the political muscle developed by left groupings in the campaigns to democratize the Labour Party during the 1970s, and especially after the 1979 defeat. Connected with this new organizational drive was a change in the social composition of city Labour Parties. By this time, the labour movement had acquired a much larger membership of public-service employees – a dominant membership in some cities. Social constituencies based on the issues of public employment, collective consumption, and cultural pluralism in a multi-ethnic city had gone some way to replacing the production-based working-class formations on which old Labourism had depended. So it was not so much that the New Left had at last found its way to a relation with the labour movement – rather, it and its base-constituencies had begun to displace it, as constituency Labour Parties acquired new white-collar memberships and new municipal class alliances were constructed.

The old arguments about old versus new class formations, class and classlessness, reappeared as political choices between the municipal strategies of Militant in Liverpool (strong on council housing and hostile to participation) and the new leadership around Ken Livingstone at the Greater London Council: strong on public transport, gender and voluntary groups, but with few material resources at its disposal to redistribute.

It is not surprising that the resonance of the new political and cultural models seems to diminish in force the further one goes from London. Finding a way of combining these old and new political formations, both within and outside the Labour Party, remains as difficult and crucial a problem as ever it has been.

Mrs Thatcher, not surprisingly, disliked the new municipal politics and has acted vigorously to put a stop to it. But Thatcherism, like the New Left, has also in turn sought to mobilize the feelings of subordinate strata about exclusion and marginalization at the hands of a perceived 'establishment' – in this case the establishment of the welfare state, including the trade unions. But some of the populist sentiments are none the less similar. Thatcherism's leading figures also represent new voices, antagonistic and resentful towards those with inherited confidence, cultural resources and power. It may be encouraging that whilst the New Left's politics did reflect the emergence of new forms of production and consumption, and the diversity and freedom of lifestyle that went with them, the culture of the New Right seems to be mainly reactive and regressive. It has the qualities of a culture of decline, even while proclaiming national and economic revival.

Whilst the right, in its attacks on economic failure, uniformity and bureaucracy, has certainly responded more effectively to social discontents and frustrations than the left has done in recent years, its culture hardly seems plausible as a mirror of the future. In its characteristic emphasis on discipline, moral certitudes, Englishness and money, it seems mainly to express reactions to anxieties provoked by social changes, not a viable way of life for a modern society. The New Left's main resource in this contest over alternative definitions and futures will still be its capacity to understand such changes and to work out their implications in political terms.

A political movement was therefore what the early New Left wanted to be, not what it was. Its failure to develop as a rooted movement, or to move the Labour Party far in that direction, have probably contributed greatly to our present political plight. Still, the aim was right, and so were many of the New Left's insights into the more pluralist and contested society which Britain was about to become. The issues and realities which it identified so clearly seem to have lost none of their political relevance.

===== 8 =====

Conference Scrapbook

During the conference, members of the early New Left offered a number of interesting reflections about their experiences in the movement, about its successes and failures, and its relation to the current crisis of the left and the rise of Thatcherism. This 'conference scrapbook' presents a few fragments from the dialogue.

A Dotted Line to Thatcherism

Clancy Sigal: I've got a hunch that there's some kind of dotted line that stretches between what we were trying to say and do and what we today call Thatcherism because, in some odd sort of way, Margaret Thatcher is the best socialist among us; that kind of fire in the belly, the depth of conviction, even the language, the type of religious impulse, was something which we once had but she now has. I think she's the shrewdest politician that we've had in this country for many, many decades.

Raphael Samuel: Mrs Thatcher's rhetoric makes the left, and particularly the independent or revolutionary left, extremely uncomfortable because a great deal of it has been appropriated from a radical language which originated in British radical nonconformity. She has turned their language against the left. It was originally libertarian socialists who attacked the big government of Whitehall in the early 1960s. It was libertarian socialists who attacked the bureaucratic management of council housing and campaigned for self-built and self-owned housing. It is a great tragedy that within the Labour Party these radical bureaucratic movements were swamped by a programme of managerial modernization. I think that we're paying the price for having allowed some of the best inheritances of a radical libertarian socialism to be used by the right. And that means one has to be extremely selective about where to counterattack the current government.

Stuart Hall: I don't apologize for one moment because we may appear to have opened the floodgates to Thatcherism in terms of what we criticized. The old agenda cannot be constituted again. We were right to criticize the old forms of nationalization and the old, deeply undemocratic, forms of the trade-union labour movement. We were right to say that when a union delivered the vote to the right or the left it delivered it in an equally undemocratic way, and that socialism cannot be rebuilt in the twenty-first century on the basis of undemocratic forms of political commitment. And we were right to criticize the forms in which welfare is delivered. That is not to say that we weren't willing to defend the welfare state. Of course we were willing to do so. You can't begin to think of socialism now without the welfare state. But we were right in saying that certain forms of the welfare state were delivered in such a bureaucratic way that large numbers of people felt in relation to them not that their rights had been expanded, but that they had been rendered passive clients. And forms of socialist welfare which make people feel like clients will never empower them; with such forms, people will never be able to take command of their material and living conditions, and the energies which drive the socialist movement will be impoverished.

*****

Spontaneity

Sheila Benson: One reason why a movement like the New Left comes to an end is that it avoids bureaucratization for too long. In order to survive, a movement must eventually bureaucratize. Yet it was the spontaneity of the New Left that was deeply appealing. There was administration: halls had to be booked for speakers, ads had to be put in the paper, the editors certainly had to get out the journal. But there wasn't a clear-cut division of labour. People rallied round to different kinds of things and split their efforts. It was amazing how through a series of phone calls, usually from Raphael Samuel, some of us could be got together to do something at the last moment. The spontaneity was attractive, although it could be a bit maddening and we sometimes made administrative blunders. But a movement that is based around spontaneity has a limited life unless it takes a decision to bureaucratize.

*****

A Rootless American

Clancy Sigal: I have always been extremely grateful for the base – for the home, in fact, – that I found as a rootless socialist American when I first came here; for the energy, the comradeship, and for that moment in the 1950s when it seemed to me, because I didn't know a hell of a lot about English history, that maybe we could kick open some doors. I certainly felt the continuity of interests between myself, as an American, and the young people who were running *ULR* and the people who were running that almost forgotten magazine *The New Reasoner*, which was absolutely brilliant. Suddenly the heart of Marxism, which had been stultifying, was broken wide open. I thought we were all engaged in a kind of collective endeavour to recapture that essential idealism, freshness, originality of an idea which had been taken away from us by the enemies of promise, by the enemies of socialism.

*****

Class and Classlessness

Stuart Hall: I agree with many of the criticisms of the early New Left, but on the question of class I make no apologies. On the question of the complexities of class, of how class relates to the current conjuncture, of the problems of class formation in Britain and why it is so difficult to organize a class and popular socialist movement, the New Left's instincts were absolutely correct. You could not possibly understand Thatcherism without understanding how – I am going to caricature it here – the traditional left, confronted by a rapidly transforming society, continued to use a descriptive language about it which was not accurate, and in which the majority of people could not see themselves reflected. Consequently, along came Thatcherism, which rooted itself in those contradictory realities and built on them the hegemony of the right. Thatcherism has been able to build a political hegemony in the fragmentation of the earlier class identities, the discontinuities between economic class position and class politics, and the way in which class identities have been cross-cut by other identities. This is exactly the problem of a sense of classlessness which we were trying to discuss. We were not talking about the fact that class had disappeared, but about the fact that class formation and class relations were being profoundly revolutionized and transformed; you couldn't have a socialist politics unless it was actually rooted in those transformations. And if socialism couldn't root itself there, horror of horrors, the right could root itself there, and bloody well has in the last eight years.

Thatcherism and the crisis of the left are not two different things; they're one and the same. Thatcherism roots itself in all those things about the English working class – how it has changed, how it has not changed – that the left will not name. As long as we go on being unable to name them, unable to face the difficulties of analysis which they pose and unable to face the transformations of the old political agendas which that brings in train, we will be inured in an analysis which was right for another period and is not right now. Other people who don't live in the past, but instead live now, will not be able to see themselves resonated in our language and will look elsewhere for political, personal, private and other kinds of solutions. That is why what Thatcherism gains is exactly what the left has not been able to do.

I'm a Modernist in this sense – not in an idiotic sense of abolishing the past, but unless socialism makes sense of the way in which people live their lives now, not only will no one vote for it, but why should anyone vote for it? If it's not inside their economies of pleasure and identification, if it doesn't speak to the fragmentation and problems which they encounter in their everyday lives, why should anybody bother when someone else is saying that they can give it to them now: 'Get on your bike! Haul yourself up by the bootstraps! Move to Docklands! Go to Tokyo! Connect yourselves to Cellnet telephones!' There are all sorts of ways to connect yourself to modernity. That's what Thatcherism is about. The problem for socialism is how genuinely to modernize society in a socialist way; how to connect socialist principles to the radically different society in which socialism must take root right now and in the next ten years.

*****

A Miner's Bible

Lawrence Daly: The thing that interested me most among the New Left economic writings, being a working miner as I was at that time, was the publication of *A Socialist Wages Plan*. It seemed to be everything I believed in. I was very much against mineworkers, or indeed any other workers, being paid purely on the basis of market forces. As a socialist, I believed that there should be a planned economy. Within the wages sector of the economy, there could be a reasonable distribution of available income based on the relative importance of the various jobs which we all do in Britain one way or another, although that does not necessarily exclude also looking at production and productivity, goods and services, supply, and everything else associated with the wider question of economics. Because I was so much impressed by *A Socialist Wages Plan*, it became for a while my Bible as an activist in the coal mines. I think that in the face of the current economic climate under Thatcherism, *A Socialist Wages Plan* should be updated and injected into discussions that are now proceeding, and thus play a part in the formation of policies that are to be presented to the electorate at the next general election.

*****

A Divided Culture

Mervyn Jones: I want to say something about the atmosphere in the New Left which to a large extent still prevails today. What seems to me to be characteristic of society at large – and what the New Left didn't succeed in escaping from – is a cultural split, or rather two cultural splits. The first is the split between the culture of science and the culture of the humanities. I use the word 'humanities' because it is a rather broader concept than the arts. The sciences have a culture of their own, and the humanities have a culture of their own, and these do not meet as they should. If you scan through the twenty-odd names of people who are speaking at this conference, you won't find any scientists. I think this is a very serious matter for the left, because increasingly over the years some of the major issues which we have had to confront require a certain scientific understanding: nuclear weapons and power, pollution and other general environmental issues. Of course we all know we are against Sizewell B, we all picket and demonstrate on the right occasions, but we don't do any more about understanding these things.

There is, I think, within the humanities a further split. In the New Left, and on the left generally, there are the artists and writers, people like Lindsay Anderson and myself, who make things, and there are the political scientists, historians, sociologists and economists – people who study and generate ideas. What worries me is that there has been little meeting of minds between the artists and the historians, sociologists, economists, and so on. At all events I am bothered by this separation. I don't believe that the friends with whom I've soldiered in the New Left throughout these twenty-five years read my novels. I read their books, but I don't think they read my novels. I don't think they've got time for that sort of thing. Certainly when we meet, we don't talk about films or theatre or novels, let alone poetry. We talk about politics, we talk about political ideas, we talk history, we talk sociology. In other words, I meet them on their ground. When I talk about literature, I talk with a totally different set of friends, my writer friends.

Now this is a sad situation, and I think that the left has not really overcome a certain attitude which regards the arts as peripheral rather than central to politics, or – something far more important than being central to politics – central to life. I am an unashamed worshipper of William Morris and of his kind of socialism. I take it that what William Morris was saying is that we are socialists because we want everybody – the whole human race – to be able to live a life in which their work is creative. He never drew any distinction between work, art, and craft. These three words were the same to William Morris. He hated capitalism because it excluded the mass of the people from fulfilling their human potential, be it as designers and creators of tangible beauty, as scholars, or as discoverers. All of us would endorse the Morris vision and the Morris ideal, but our endorsement is rather unconvincing if any field of creativity is excluded from our own interest.

*****

The Virtue of Openness

Raphael Samuel: One of the things I feel most sympathetic towards in the old New Left was its openness. Openness meant that the New Left was taken up and transformed repeatedly by intellectual movements and mass movements not of its own making. There is no reference to nuclear disarmament in our first editorial for *Universities and Left Review*, but it was CND which transformed the whole meaning that we gave to what a new politics could be. Similarly, there is no reference to popular culture or working-class communities in issue 1 of *ULR*. In fact, culturally it was of a piece with *Left Review* and Communist publications of the 1940s. Yet by issue 2 we had a symposium on working-class community. What transformed it was, quite simply, Hoggart's *The Uses of Literacy*, and an unknown tutor-organizer for the Extramural Department who sent us in an article just before our first issue – Raymond Williams. That imaginative breakthrough didn't come from us, but it did register itself on the New Left.

*****

Workers' Control

Lawrence Daly: I have never been an advocate of workers' control of industry. I believe in community control of industry. I think that the miner, along with everyone else, is a consumer at the same time, and his interest as a consumer has to be taken into account. For there to be real or actual democratic control of industry, we have to find a means by which workers with the necessary technical qualifications – I am not in favour of the most popular guy in the coal mine running the industry if he doesn't know one end of a safety device from the other – combine with management to make the economic decisions that determine the future of the industry, taking into consideration everyone's interests, including the interests of the man who produces the coal. That means that almost everyone working in the industry, even if he is just a clerical worker or a technical supervisor, has some control. I think that there is still room for discussion of this problem and that – trying to avoid being nostalgic – in the late 1950s the New Left made a great beginning, not just in a general political sense but in the one industry that I do know. Its members were coming forward with new ideas that could still form the basis for an economic strategy necessary for what we could describe as a truly free, democratic socialist society.

*****

Green Politics

Malcolm McEwen: I was one of the founders of *The New Reasoner* and one of the first editors of the *New Left Review,* but I didn't stay with them very long. One of the reasons I didn't stay with them was because I was branching out in a completely new direction – a direction that has not, as far as I know, been mentioned today. It doesn't appear to have figured in the consciousness of the New Left to any degree at all. That is the whole question of resource conservation. The ideology of labourism and communism and also the New Left – they are all the same – was that they all believed that you have to find the right mechanism by which you can maximize growth in the economy and then ensure proper distribution. And that, of course, raises all sorts of power questions about the workers, consumers, and the like. I don't disagree with much that has been said – very little indeed – but it does seem to me that there is a huge element that is missing.

Cultural Practices

Trevor Griffiths: The deepest resonance of the New Left for me was in those formative five years from 1957 to 1962. It has something to do with the key notion of culture not being a thing which is made by and for small elites, privileged and prestigious and status-ridden, but instead being about whole societies: culture is about whole social practices. A particular emphasis not on proletarianism but certainly on working-class culture was also evident – a preoccupation with linking theoretical and practical discourse. The New Left also pointed out something else to me, though it is hard at this distance to know whether it was saying it on its own and uniquely or whether that was part of the air that you were breathing between, say, 1957 and 1962. It looked at the arts or art as a transitive process rather than as a self-expressive and self-referring process. There was always a sense that there was an audience out there with whom communication was about to take place.

I developed my own rather self-conscious writing practice in those five years, and I think there were things about the New Left and its cultural theory that helped me to do that. It helped me to deconstruct, to some extent, the notion of the artist as autonomous, as self-referring, as wholly able to solve the problem as if that problem existed on a page and not out there in life. It helped me to see the writing of a dramatic text, for example, as very much a dialectical process between a single sensibility, a single voice, and large numbers of claims that lay outside that single voice and that single life trajectory. What the New Left was also saying at the time, which has been important to me, is that you actually have to get stuck in; it is a bit like the Brecht bit that 'you cannot work in a sewer and refuse to handle shit'. I take that to mean that if there are structures of power within the society and culture, then they have to be attacked in fairly direct ways, and part of that attack will be to use those structures of power for subversive purposes. That certainly has been an idea I have carried with me, and it may well have had its founding moment for me in those formative five years and in the work that was done then.

*****

Cultural Capital

Raphael Samuel: In some ways the New Left may have been part of what it attacked. The very idea of four Oxford graduates setting out to teach socialism to the world comes from the particular vanity of this university, which was mercifully undermined by the later student movement of 1968, but I think we wouldn't have had the arrogance to embark on this project if we had not been the beneficiaries of a century of accumulated moral, symbolic and cultural capital that this university had.

Stuart Hall: In a wholly unconscious and unthinking way, we occupied our position somewhere at the summit of the British higher-education system without ever asking how on earth we had got there and why it was our destiny to produce these new things. The degree to which we were totally unreflective about that really terrifies me in retrospect.

*****

A 'Popular Front'

Lindsay Anderson: The best way to formulate the issue at hand would be to ask: What connection is there between the New Left and art? I think this is particularly apt for people who spend their time professionally in the arts: the longer you live, the more you put art first. I am not using the word 'art' in any pretentious way. I mean simply the professional practice of whatever particular art you happen to be concerned with – in my case film and theatre direction. This distinction is important, because as an artist one is not necessarily political; as a human being one is political but as an artist one doesn't sit around spending one's time thinking about how I can ensure that my creative work plays its part in the New Left. That would be ridiculous.

If one is going to talk in any useful way as an artist, one has by definition to speak personally; so let me say what, from my experience, really happened all those years ago. I had been concerned with making some documentary films towards the end of the fifties and launching a programme at the National Film Theatre which we labelled a 'movement' and called 'Free Cinema'. The extraordinary and encouraging thing was to receive an approach from two people, Ralph Samuel and Stuart Hall, who were organizers of the seminal New Left which really started in the universities – Oxford and Cambridge – with a magazine called *Universities and Left Review* (which has fossilized, I suppose, into the *New Left Review* of today).

1956 was, in retrospect, a fantastic year. We had Suez, we had Hungary, we had our modest little movement of Free Cinema at the

National Film Theatre, we had the opening of the English Stage Company at the Royal Court and the first performance of *Look Back in Anger*. Independent television started at very much the same time. It was a terrifically stimulating period of shake-up after the congealed social situation of post-war and the first half of the fifties. So it was quite in the spirit of the time that when we made our documentary films – I made a film called *Every Day Except Christmas* about the Covent Garden market, which was shown at the National Film Theatre – we received an overture from the *Universities and Left Review*. It was the political (or social) people who wanted to make connections and be friendly. It was surprising and very, very encouraging – because it suddenly seemed as if there could really be a 'Popular Front' of political and creative principle; and in that popular front, movies and theatre could have a place and enjoy sympathetic support. For just a short time that is what actually happened.

Of course, that was a time when socialism was a word that could still be used – unlike today. It was a time when there was an establishment tradition that was so rigid and so out of date that it encouraged a healthy spirit of opposition. It was a time when it was possible to be an artist of, shall we say, progressive temperament and feel that there was an equivalent or sympathetic political movement with which one could, if not completely identify, at least ally oneself, and to which one could look for support. Thirty years later, by my experience, the situation has changed. I don't now believe in any real connection between my artistic and creative work and any political or social group, party or movement.

Is this the fault of the New Left? Or of the left? Or of myself as an artist? I suppose politicians would blame the artists for not putting themselves at the service of the 'movement', while the artists, who are traditionally sceptical of political involvement, would not bother to blame anybody. I would suggest only that the political leftists, after that brief, delightful period when they saw politics and culture as significantly related, have fallen back into the characteristic English habit of thinking of art in elitist, minority terms, favouring the exotic products of the foreigner over the dreary attempts of the native.

This is certainly true of the cinema. I realized that an era had ended when I picked up a copy of the *New Left Review* and found it featuring an (yet another) examination of the work of Hitchcock – and I mean, of course, the American, not the British Hitchcock. American vitality and money have licked the British cinema. The 'New British Cinema' of Channel Four inspiration is intermittently lively, but certainly not radical (with one or two very lonely exceptions). And our 'film academics' continue to promote, on extravagant subsidy, an idea of cinema dehumanized, insignificant – and irrelevant.

And the theatre: does anyone now remember the posters which announced the opening of the National Theatre on the South Bank? 'The Theatre of the People' was the slogan – or something like that. What a sad laugh! No, as far as theatre and cinema go, we are back in the mid fifties. The movement petered out: middle-class, conformist, commercial values have prevailed. Britain is different, of course; but the same. When I look around me today, and listen to all the clever spouting, I can envisage nothing more clearly than Maggie's Fourth Term.

Then and Now:
A Re-evaluation of the
New Left

In this edited transcript of the final session of the conference, three of the founding editors of *Universities and Left Review*, Charles Taylor, Raphael Samuel and Stuart Hall, offer their critical evaluations of the early New Left and respond to questions. (Only questioners who were active in the early New Left have been identified.)

Presentations

Charles Taylor: I'd like to take off from a single idea brought up in one of the previous sessions – that we don't really know what we mean by socialism. Or put it this way: we used to talk as though we had a very clear idea, and now we're not so sure.

Why do we find it so difficult to know what we are talking about when we talk about socialism? I think the reason why we find it hard to come up with a quick formula – or even a slow formula – is the crippling belief, very deeply rooted in the socialist tradition, perhaps mainly in the Marxist tradition, that there is a major systemic change that we could bring about between capitalism and socialism which would, by the same stroke, overcome a number of very deep human woes, problems, divisions, and so on. The difficulty of thinking out a new definition of socialism is that very often people have that requirement in their minds: that we're thinking of the definition of a new kind of society in which these problems and difficulties would be answered together. And the reason why that is crippling is that I don't think there is such a thing.

I would just like to mention, in the first part of my remarks, three dilemmas which point to certain deep human difficulties, the solutions to which don't fit easily together.

First, there are two big sides to the traditional socialist movement. On the one hand, you could think of it as a great protest against the domination and exploitation of some people by others; on the other, it was also a movement that had the aspiration to much greater self-rule. It was thought that there was a systemic change that would somehow bring about both those changes together, and that's what socialism was. Of course we have startling and horrifying examples of societies which have

145

at least claimed to have done away with exploitation, in the capitalist sense of the word, but have failed miserably in terms of self-rule. They are worse than the Western liberal societies. Nevertheless, we are fixed on the idea that these two goals should go together.

In market societies today, systemic features keep certain people in a very deprived condition in all sorts of ways, not just economically. The line between those who are in this position and those who are not is not the same as the line between those who are employed by capitalist firms and those who are not. There is some overlap, but basically we are talking about two different things. So in our society today, the very structure of industry and the structure of employment in both the private and public sectors (and the key to this is, in a sense, the private sector) is a very top–down one that continues to disempower people.

The thrust towards greater self-rule therefore implies one obvious possible constituency and an obvious set of objectives: namely, bringing about greater control in the workplace, and so on. This would have to come about through greater public ownership. But the whole question of exploitation, the way in which the system marginalizes certain people and keeps them in pockets of deprivation, is not the same problem: it does not concern the same group of people; it is not the same constituency mobilized, and so on. The solution to one problem could easily come about without the other being properly addressed.

There is a second dilemma, which involves the question of how we reconcile the freedom we want to give to individuals and to self-governing groups on the one hand, with the requirements of solidarity on the other. We can see this tension acted out in the economic sphere.

Once we get away from too-simple views about planning, which I confess we all shared, and once we take the point – which I think has now been driven home with undeniable clarity – that any model socialist economy requires an important role for the market, then certain difficulties remain. For example, one of the things which brought about Thatcherism in 1979 was, I believe, the 'winter of discontent'. One of the things that brought that about was the collapse of some kind of wages policy. Now I don't necessarily argue that the particular policy that collapsed was the best one, or that it couldn't have been better handled, but I do want to take issue with the argument that I've heard people on the left make since then: that a wages policy is an attempt to address a capitalist problem that socialists don't have to consider. I think that's just an illusion. We would have that kind of problem under any conceivable regime. Here the crippling of our thought about a socialist future cripples our thought about policy within present-day capitalist society. We very often talk as though the tension between these two goals – freedom on the one hand, and solidarity on the other – is simply a problem for capitalist society, and as though we would get over this if we had a socialist society.

The third dilemma stems from the rise of a number of new social movements and sensibilities. For example, we've had a tremendous revolution in consciousness around the question of feminism in the last thirty years. It's clear that the feminism that was in existence then – and indeed had been for a century before – was quite different from the feminism that exists today around issues of identity and gender construction – an issue our civilization has put on the agenda over the last thirty years, a huge issue which wasn't a problem faced before. It just isn't inscribed in the clouds somewhere that the way this issue is going to be faced, and ought most humanly to be worked out, will necessarily lie on the same lines, and be easily combinable, with the solutions to the other things that I mentioned earlier.

The same sort of remark goes for the ecological restraints that we have to impose on all modern economies. Once again, an economy could be socialist in the sense of overcoming exploitation and allowing for a certain amount of self-rule, and it could solve miraculously the dilemmas of freedom and solidarity; this society could be one in which the problem of gender identity had been faced squarely and people had come to some solution about it, and it could still be a society which ravages the environment, which will lead to a sticky end.

So these are several dilemmas where we have to think out what we want to do without the a priori certainty that there's a thing called socialism – like a parlour game: find the answer. We must stop pretending that there's a thing called socialism that will solve all these things together at one stroke, now. If we play that parlour game we shall never, never get an answer.

There are two other things I wanted to say. One concerns the problem of our class analysis. We have to think of it in two senses – particularly, perhaps, in Britain. There's the analysis of class in the sense of the analysis of the extent to which society is hag-ridden with divisions of status and consciousness and so on. Then there's the analysis of class, more in the line of the traditional Marxist meaning of the term, in which you analyse the power base of society. First, these two questions very often have to be separated – although they can be interrelated. Secondly, the second kind of analysis has to be rethought in a way which must liberate us from Marxism as such, because the picture of the 'working class' as what stands over against the 'ruling class', as the underpinning for several of the problems I have sketched out here, seems to me to be just so wildly improbable and beside the point that it is better to drop it. So the a priori that we have to drop, which corresponds to the a priori of the simple solution, is the a priori of a single class analysis.

Next, we have to face another set of problems to do with the new international order. What you'd want to see is a kind of new international economic order – and we haven't really even begun to think out what it involves to have such an order in the absence of a world socialist state. I'll stop there: let's just put that on the agenda.

Raphael Samuel: Possibly apocryphally, Mao Tse-tung, being questioned by French journalists sometime in the 1960s, was asked what he thought about the French Revolution of 1789, and he replied with proper Marxist prudence that it was too early to judge yet. I am sure that's right for any kind of judgement on the New Left – both because, as we know, history is constantly being remade, and also because some elements in the New Left are still growing; they are a creative force in British society now. I'd like to mention three which happen to interest me in particular.

One which somehow got buried in the later 1960s was libertarianism. I've been very impressed rereading not only *The New Reasoner* and *Universities and Left Review* but also a journal which helped me through the mid sixties, which were rather bleak years from the radical point of view: *Anarchy*. I have been struck with how much of the cultural revolution of the 1960s was actually prefigured in that journal, which was running in easy tandem with a larger New Left. I think there are questions raised within the libertarian wing of the New Left that could still repay attention.

Secondly, Marxism – which seems to me to be a very live intellectual tradition in this country, and is certainly infinitely preferable as a way of understanding contemporary capitalism, enterprise culture or Thatcherism to the various forms of conspiracy theory or moralistic talks of betrayal which are otherwise on offer on the left. Whenever I feel gloomy about politics, I think of Marx's 11th thesis on Feuerbach – the philosophers have only interpreted the world; the point is to change it – and then think also that one can have consolation from reversing it – if we can't actually change the world, the least we can do is to understand it.

A third point is the originally antipolitical bias, the deep impatience with a sense of suffocation by conventional party politics and party leaderships. The sense that it is in civil society, and not in high politics, that momentous changes take place is surely far more true now with the demise of mass parties. In the 1950s they were still a transitional form of church. Today they are empty shells.

At the same time – while remembering, I hope, Mao's caution – I do have a sense of ending on two counts. One is very general – I won't rehearse the argument again: about 'concerned' middle-class radicalism. I think this was a phenomenon which crystallized in the 1950s and that many of the liberalizations of British society are due to it, but I have a sense that its utility may be coming to an end. In particular the way in which it got caught up with Labour Party politics in the last ten years has been a disaster for the Labour Party and, as a matter of fact, for middle-class radicalism itself – a form of politics in which Labour's middle-class recruits set out to impersonate the imaginary voice of the masses. Here I look back with some pleasure on the freshness of the early New Left. At least, whatever the limitations, whatever our blindnesses, it does seem to me that people were actually saying what they thought, not pretending to speak in the name of absentee or nonexistent constituencies.

Another point where I feel a sense of ending is in relation to counter-culture. Mike Rustin said in an earlier discussion that you can live your whole life today within a radical culture, and I fear he is right. In all the attempts from the 1950s onwards to create an alternative culture, we created a home which in the end became a prison. I think many people in different ways have felt, as I myself have since the Falklands War, that all those things which had been painfully built up actually insulated us from public feeling. I am strongly in disagreement with *Marxism Today,* and in disagreement with some of the things Stuart has been saying. But I think that the effort – Stuart's in particular – to break out of the ghetto, and speak to a reality other than one created for our own comfort, is a brave one and absolutely what socialism should be about. So I myself am very unhappy with the idea of creating something which, as it were, encloses us.

I end by saying something about socialism and what Charles Taylor said about a priori socialism. I'm a lifelong socialist, but I actually lost faith in socialism about thirty years ago, in the sense that I haven't wanted to live in a socialist society since sometime about the mid fifties. If I thought we were about to have a socialist Britain, I am not at all sure what, as a socialist, I would feel about it. My heart wouldn't rejoice. What I care about is a socialist movement. What I care about is socialism as a metaphor for solidarity, for opposition, and for collectivism. Obviously I would like Britain to be a society in which there wasn't a Conservative Party: other countries seem to manage quite satisfactorily without one. One of the things you need a socialist movement for is to combat Toryism. I don't believe that what has sustained the very rich socialist movement that there's been in this country has been only, or exclusively, or even mainly, a vision of the future. Quite often it's been a way of keeping faith with a past – both a real past and an imaginary past.

One of the advances made by socialists – and, as a matter of fact, within British society – in the last thirty years is a decreasing willingness to postpone to some notional or mythical tomorrow things that are needed in the here and now. That's what I think of as the great gain that was made by the liberation movements of the 1960s and 1970s, and particularly by the women's movement. There's a phrase which Stuart introduced into the rhetoric of the old *Universities and Left Review*: talking about 'socialism in the here and now'. People are now much more impatient with what they demand. They say that if you're to be a socialist, then you actually have to prove your credentials by what you do now: by what you do if you're in a council, if you're in a school, if you're in a college, or if you're in the Labour Party or in a CND group. That seems to me to be a great gain in clear-sightedness – and, as a matter of fact, in honesty in politics.

Stuart Hall: In thinking about this session, I've been trying to hoist myself around from facing the past to thinking about the present and the future. I agree with a great deal that people have been saying about what the New Left didn't do, and couldn't bring off, what we didn't see or what we were blind to, and so on. In spite of that, I don't think I've ever thought of describing myself in any other way than as belonging to the New Left. This must mean something in terms of the present conjuncture, even though I'm probably not a member of the New Left in the way that I was at the time we're talking about, and I've never set a great deal of store by trying to prove my absolute practical consistency. But what are the things that give my commitment to the space defined by the New Left that kind of continuity for me? I'll just try to identify some.

The first is the point I made in the opening talk this morning. I think there was then, and always will be, a space for radical politics which is neither Stalinist nor social-democratic. Somewhere between the old forms of social democracy and the old forms of Stalinism is the space in which a new politics and a new socialist agenda can be constructed. I thought that then, I think that now, and I would like you to think so too. The third space; the other route. This position often overlaps, and is often confused with, other positions with which we often have to make alliances. Nevertheless, it is a distinct political space. Today we've been trying, in a very uneven and perhaps to some extent unhelpful way, to define for you what it was, at a certain historical moment, to try to live that political space. It lays on us, in relation to contemporary ideas and contemporary political struggles, the injunction still to try to find and define a political space which is articulated in opposition to those two constituted positions on the left. That is the project of the New Left.

The second has to do with something which I think was implicit in what the New Left did, though it was by no means always explicit. It was probably often lived unconsciously, and certainly not agreed as a matter of a common agenda: the notion that socialism can mean something for us and generations to come only if its project is radically remade; not dug out of the cupboard, dusted off and slightly glossed and put back in place, but actually rethought from the bottom up. That is an extremely difficult and agonizing political process to go through, because it means junking a whole number of commitments and allegiances. It means not thinking in old ways, it means letting go of certain political habits, it means exposing your most cherished ideas to the remorseless process that Marx called 'the real movement of history'. I don't want to use the Thatcherite metaphor, but it does mean, politically, pulling yourself up from the inside. Nevertheless, I do think that is what the challenge before socialism means now. The New Left, in its own fumbling way and in its own historical time, incorporated such a project of the 'historic renewal of socialism and the left'.

The third point I want to make is that this process of renewal is always, and has to be, profoundly rooted in the realities of the present. Gramsci said: 'Turn your face violently towards things as they exist now.' Not as you'd like them to be, not as you think they were ten years ago, not as they're written about in the sacred texts, but as they really are: the contradictory, stony ground of the present conjuncture. There isn't any already fully remade 'Socialist Man', with whom the New Dawn is going to be made. There is no utopia lying beyond the revolution which would be totally different from anything you know now. The subjects of socialism are just ordinary folks, just like you and me, just as confused, partly remade, partly ancient. That is the only material of which a new kind of society is made. And unless one can find ways of actually grounding any kind of socialist language, or utopia, or prospect for the future, in that contradictory reality where we are now, I don't see any hope for it.

That's not a very optimistic statement, because I do believe that in some way 'the real movement of history' has left the language of socialism and socialist analysis behind. Socialism is now so often anachronistically fixed to descriptions of the world which are out of date. And it is not surprising, if our descriptions of the world are out of date, that we cannot project a possible future – a future which would be different from how we live now, but which people can see as building on how they live now. That rooting of politics in the realities of the present is, I think, an extremely difficult thing to bring about, but I know of no other way in which to do it; and it seems to me that although the New Left didn't understand self-consciously what it was doing, when it was good it was trying to turn its face to that contradictory terrain that history has produced as the only soil out of which some alternative society can emerge.

The next point is that the New Left contributed to – though in no sense completed – an expansion of the definition of what politics is about. It helped to transform that narrow, confined, institutionally limited notion of 'the political'. I think it only just began that important job. An occasion like this does almost oblige us to say either that everything was done then by the New Left, or that nothing was done. I just want to say that *some things* were done then, though a lot of important questions about which socialism must be concerned were not asked. Without in any way excusing or letting ourselves off the hook, I refuse to indulge in the anachronistic game of blaming the New Left for not doing what the 1980s have only with extreme difficulty discovered. That anachronism – coupled, as it often is, to the moralism of blame and sectarian rectitude and self-righteousness – is worse than useless (some of it has been much in evidence today) and I refuse it; I will have nothing whatsoever to do with it.

I very much agreed with some of the emphases in what Charles Taylor was saying, though I don't agree with many of the others. It would take a very different occasion, with a quite different agenda, to create the context for a debate about what the actual analysis of contemporary capitalist society is, and what its characteristic social forces and tendencies are, and we could probably not now agree about that. But I thought he made an underlying point with which I very profoundly agree. It has to do with the diversity of experiences and of identities which are the ground of contemporary politics.

Now I think the New Left – partly symptomatically, partly in its analysis – understood that somehow any kind of socialist or radical movement would be constructed out of difference, and in that sense was rooted in a recognition of differences. It understood that people no longer experience society through a simple identity – not even a class identity, important as questions of class still are. There were different identities, different forms of social subjectivity, which had to be mobilized in any kind of contemporary political movement. The New Left in no sense completed that analysis, but I think that is one of the ways in which I would say, as between the first time I called myself a socialist and now, that something in my own political subjectivity has radically shifted. I owe this shift to two things: my involvement in the politics of ethnicity and race, and the influence of feminism and sexual politics – both unthinkable except in terms of the construction of political positions through and across difference.

The problem now is to rethink the politics of class as, and through, a politics of difference. I clearly did for a time believe that it was not me but 'Socialist Man' who would appear somewhere, homogenize all the differences, and 'make socialism'. That's related to Chuck's one single moment – the revolutionary apocalypse – after which everything else would fall into place. 'Socialist Man' has gone over the hill and far away, and thank God for his departure. *Finito!* Now any future is a future of difference, any future society is a society of diversity where people will agree on a common ground of political mobilization which doesn't refuse or deny the difference.

In short – to quote Gramsci again – politics is a 'war of position': a hegemonic political strategy. Some things that recur in my memory of the New Left prefigured that form of politics. Some people talked about it in terms of 'openness', the hatred of sectarianism; others talked about it in terms of political indecision. It was probably both, but at any rate it allowed the voices of quite different experiences, quite different senses of oppression, to come into the political debate, to make some stab at shaping the political agenda. That was, politically, something quite new on the left.

The last point I want to make is this. The New Left did mark, in my view, the end – really the end – of the belief that socialism would come about as a result of the inexorable laws of history, or the purely objective historical contradictions built into capitalism, and deliver the new age behind men's and women's backs. It wasn't an entirely voluntaristic politics, but it did know that socialism was either made or it wouldn't happen at all. If you don't construct a strategy for change, it won't happen. No one knows this better than Mrs Thatcher. If enough people don't get into the building of it, there is no other engine – not God, Marx, capital, the working class, the vanguard party, or anything else that will deliver socialism for you on a plate.

Now, in that sense the New Left was not a socialism of the will, but it was a socialism of what I call 'the social imaginary'. Raphael Samuel talked about the libertarian element, and I would talk about the utopian element, in the New Left. I don't see a socialist politics of any kind arising in this country which cannot capture the 'social imaginary', which is unable to talk about transcendence, about the political, social and cultural realities towards which people are moving. If we remain locked into the language of the present, the left will become a footnote in the onward march of modernity.

Questions and Responses

Question 1: *We are talking here about two spaces. Stuart Hall talked about the space between social democracy and Stalinism. Charles Taylor talked about the space between individualism or capitalism and the general will. The question that bothers me is: are we talking about the same space at different levels of abstraction, or are those two different*

*spaces? My own feeling is – since I believe that the first (Stuart Hall's)
space does exist, and the other doesn't – that it is not the same thing.*

Charles Taylor (response to Question 1): I think you are right, it is not
the same thing. The space that Stuart is talking about is a space in which
the socialist movement can find itself and orientate itself, but I am talking, perhaps at a more utopian level, about a space in which a future
society could live. Now in that sense it doesn't exist, but I think you have
a stronger claim there: you'd want to say that it can't exist. It seems to
me that Stuart's claim is about the kind of movement we want to live in
now, and work in now, and orientate ourselves upon now, and I am talking about the kind of bases of a self-governing society that I see we
could build.

First Questioner: *Can I change the question to ask in what sense you see
a connection between the two spaces?*

Charles Taylor: I think there is a connection because, from my point of
view, the way I would define the middle space that Stuart talks about is
very much animated by my view of that third space in terms of the
society we're working towards. But I think we'd get all sorts of disagreements on the panel and in the room because we are steering by different
images of socialism. There is a relation, but they're distinct.

Stuart Hall (response to Question 1): I think my response is not all that
different from Charles Taylor's. There are two different things, probably
at two different levels of abstraction. I do see a connection between the
two, and I was trying to suggest that connection myself when I talked
about what I called the 'third space' politically, between Stalinism and
social democracy, linking it with the last point about diversity, difference
and choice. However, what I mean by 'difference' is not quite the same
as what Chuck seems to mean by 'individualization'. Nevertheless there
is a sense in which the other forms of collective solidarity don't seem to
me any longer quite in place, either as the ground for a contemporary
politics or as the appropriate imagery for a socialist utopia. So in my
own political thinking, I am trying to see whether it is possible to think
about a society which is not wholly driven back into private, atomized,
fragmented individualism but which understands its commitments and
solidarities to forms of mobilized collective action as always conditional,
never complete, always operating through difference.

That is what I meant by the end of 'Socialist Man'. To be a socialist
now is to be a socialist with questions: it is to be a socialist in the under-

standing that to be a socialist is also to be a feminist, and that feminism interrogates socialism in a very profound way. It is also, for me, to be black, which interrogates thought in the categories and in relation to the experience of 'the West' in very profound ways. In that sense our political commitments are now bound to be provisional or contingent in ways in which they have not customarily been. That is how I try to think the space in which the socialist project could be renewed: taking the pressure of the irreversible movements in contemporary society, and indeed around the world, towards greater diversity, greater openness, greater choice, and therefore in some senses, greater fragmentation.

But it's not only fragmentation as loss. There are also gains: the recognition of the fact that there is no politics which will so dissolve difference that people won't retain a sense of their own individual material and cultural location. I think that is increasingly what socialist politics will be like, and is itself a response to a changing material and social reality. In a sense it is probably what it was always like, except that we had no language in which actually to describe the real diversity of socialist movements, or indeed of 'class experience'. In that sense, I try to connect the two without being able to fold them neatly into one another.

Question 2: *It seems to me that there is a convergence of opinion amongst the three of you about what socialism means now. In his remarks, Raphael Samuel was talking about the extent to which socialism should be understood as a movement of perpetual opposition which breeds forms of co-operation and other good things that we definitely want – but he seems to suggest that when it goes beyond the state of perpetual opposition to become empowered politically, that might not be such a good thing. Stuart Hall talked about the extent to which socialism had to recognize the fact of human plurality, and said that any sort of intelligent politics has to start from the fact that people are fundamentally different and that there are different concerns voiced from different parts of society that in the end might not be able to be reconciled. Earlier on today, Charles Taylor talked about the need for decentralization and the extent to which a sort of global political vision, perhaps articulated around a political party's programme, might be in opposition to this need for decentralization.*

I think a lot of us in this room are compelled by some of what these different strands of basically the same argument say. But on the other hand – and this is the question I would like to put to the speakers – to what extent does the type of socialist politics that you are all talking about also have the following concomitant flaw: by shunning party politics because of its totalizing vision, to what extent are we not, from the very outset, disempowering ourselves, or admitting that we can go only so far in implementing a certain set of political conceptions and policies?

Question 3: *I'm a member of the so-called New Right. I'm very familiar with the literature of the New Left and the classical left, and come to meetings like this on the basis of 'know thine enemy'. But when I read this stuff, I don't have the sense that I have an enemy at all, because a lot of the arguments that I'm putting across, and the roots of my politics, are not addressed. Journals like* Marxism Today *and a lot of other current leftist journals talk about the New Right as though it's just constituted of old right ideas.*

In none of the magazines or journals I've come across, or any particular recent books, have matters such as the property-rights movement been addressed, or Austrian economics, public-choice school, or more recent works of social and economic history. Also I'm amazed that Charles Taylor still talks in terms of a world socialist state and that most Marxists are still not familiar with, or do not understand, the 'economic calculation argument' – one of the most basic roots of my arguments against Marxism – and yet a lot of people have not even heard of it. Now whether or not you want to shoot me down on my particular politics, I'm not particularly bothered, but I would like to know from the panel: Why are these arguments not being addressed? Why haven't these questions entered into your journals and books? I just don't see myself as having an opposition. I've got nobody to argue with.

Question 4 [Mervyn Jones]: *What people have said in the course of the day reminds me very much of something from the Marx Brothers. I'm now going back to the sequence in* Go West *in which the Marx Brothers are in charge of this train which they've got to take across the prairie. And they're running out of fuel, they're running into danger, so they say 'Right, we break up the train'. And they start to break up first the rear coach, and then the next coach . . . you remember all this, I'm sure. So, as I was listening to Chuck, his whole journey lasted only ten minutes: first of all we broke up the planned economy; then we broke up wage demands; then, if I understood it correctly, we burnt up Marxism, and we finished by burning up the working class. So the question, seriously, I want to ask is: What accommodation have we still got for people who want to travel?*

Charles Taylor: To what Mervyn Jones said: yes, some of these things I genuinely did burn up. I burnt up the Marxism car first. But the others, I don't mean to burn up; I just meant to point out that we need to have that car but it's pulling in another direction, it's pulling on another track from another car – that we always have to have some kind of difficult adjustment. We can't give up planning; that would be an absurdity. The idea that planning can solve all our problems we gave up a long time ago – at whatever point we accepted, for instance, that markets are central for socialism. So that means there are certain standing dilemmas that we are going to be in, that society is in now, and we have to think through our way of dealing with them. That is what thinking through socialism is. And the corresponding attitude of not realizing that – which is that we face the dilemmas today by saying 'well, that's a problem for capitalist society; it wouldn't occur in socialism' – we must abandon for ever, and face these problems today. So these other cars haven't been thrown away, but the idea that they're on a single train is abandoned. We have to rewrite the Marx Brothers' script.

Can I just say a word about the second question? This may be where I don't entirely agree with everybody here. To extend the earlier metaphor, I think we ought to be running several trains to different destinations at the same time and try to make a timetable that will make sense in the end. I don't really want to abandon this idea of being a member of a party which can take government in the polity which I'm in, but I don't think that's going to bring socialism, no matter how good the party is. There have to be very profound changes at other levels – including, for example, people who take their fate in their own hands, where industries have closed down, and make some sort of co-operative out of it, and similar kinds of movements. There has to be all that together, but one essential part of it is this political-party activity at the centre. I think this is essential not only because you need certain legislative changes; I think also that if you abandon that domain to other political movements altogether, you are also opening the society to certain kinds of barbarization that you could otherwise fight back. So I'd like to be on several levels at once, and this is where there may be a difference between what Raph's saying and what I'm saying.

And very briefly with respect to the third question – I hadn't heard of all the things you mentioned. I don't know, for instance, what *the* 'economic calculation argument' is. I have heard several of them, but I don't know what *the* one is. I know some of them, and where I come from we argue against them all the time – like rational-choice theory. When I was last in Chicago we had quite a vigorous discussion on this, and if it's my opinion that Marxism is not entirely adequate in some of the ways I've given here, when you get to rational-choice theory having anything to do with human life – well!

Raphael Samuel (response to Question 2): The idea of building a socialism, or a politics, on difference corresponds very well with a particular

post-Modernist aesthetic and with certain real, felt fragmentations which
have been experienced in British life in the last thirty years, so to
that extent it corresponds to a common sense of present-day British
sensibility. But it is actually a very partial understanding. There actually
is a systematic, continuous duality in the way in which we see ourselves:
on the one hand we are defined by our difference and our particularity;
but on the other there are no less compelling – in fact very often more
imaginatively compelling – notions which stress what we have in
common with others. And the left, or sections of the left, have tried to
wish sentiments of nationality, whether political nationality or cultural
nationalism, away to our own satisfaction, but not to that of the great
majority of our fellow-citizens, or of peoples in other countries, who
obstinately adhere to a notion, imaginatively compelling even if it
doesn't correspond to individual experience, of some larger collectivity.

I think that the particular disasters of the Labour left in the last few
years have not come from championing minority causes. It has been a
great gain that it should do so, for the excellent reason Stuart gave – that
in fact labour movements have always been defending highly diverse
interests, albeit apparently under a common politics. What has been a
disaster is not finding a majoritarian language with which to advocate
those causes for others. The miners' strike would be, I think, a very good
example where there was a very substantial minority of national opinion
in strong support of the miners, for a great variety of reasons – by no
means necessarily or even usually the same as that of the miners themselves. Yet even in the miners' support groups, there was no kind of
reaching towards some other language in which the Labour Party or the
trade-union movement or individual miner support groups could advocate that in ways that might command a majority support in the country.

I believe the same thing is true in anti-racism, where there are really
very deep sentiments derived sometimes from Christian universalism,
sometimes from everyday experience, from many different discourses in
this country that could be mobilized – should be mobilized for a multi-
national, multi-ethnic society. Unfortunately, the only kind of language
that has been used on the whole by Labour councils is one of 'rights'.
The abandonment of an attempt to find a majority language that would
include a majority language of politics, of country and of class is a disaster for any kind of politics, whether it's socialist or not – certainly for
the Labour Party, but also for socialism. So, I think you can have both a
much greater appreciation of division and yet a sense of common cause,
because if there isn't a larger sense of common cause, then there actually
isn't a public politics at all.

Question 5: *I would like to say briefly how I think the class nature of* *society has profoundly changed. The recognition of this seems to me a presupposition of any clear socialist thinking for the future.*

There was a conception of the working class in the past which wasn't quite accurate with respect to the reality of the past, but which it was then possible to sustain because it was sufficiently close to that reality. With a bit of political enthusiasm you could sustain it. Now it is patently unsustainable. In that past conception, the working class had four characteristics. They were – in the phrase of Das Kapital, *Volume 1 – 'the immense majority of society'. Secondly, they were the people who produced the wealth of society, on whom therefore the rest of society depended: in the words of the famous working-class American song, 'Solidarity For Ever': 'Without our brain and muscle, not a single wheel can turn'. Thirdly, they were the exploited people; they were, to put exploitation in simple form, the people who put in more hours than were contained in what they were able to consume. And finally, they were the deprived people, the people who were the poorest in society.*

Now those were four characteristics, logically independent, conceived as coalescing in one group. When you get those four characteristics together, politically it is absolute dynamite, because you've got the power to change society that comes from the first two characteristics – the fact that you're the immense majority and the fact that you're the producer upon whom everybody depends. And you've got the motivation to change society from the second two characteristics – the fact that you are exploited and so deprived.

Many people say that there was never a group that had those four characteristics, that there's nothing new in the fact that they don't coalesce. But the degree of dissociation of those characteristics is far greater today than it has ever been before, and you can see that in politics which attach themselves to one or another of these characteristics: post-left politics. You get majoritarian politics: we can't pretend that the working class is a majority, so we need a new majority; we get a rainbow coalition of different sorts of groups. Then you get people who focus on productionism as such: you can't pretend that it's just exploited and deprived people who coincide with the producers, but what we want is producers as such, so you get the Wilson 'white heat of technology', and you get an article written in the Guardian *one week after the last Labour election defeat, saying our mistake was not to address ourselves to the data-processors and high-tech people. You get people who say: 'we don't understand why you socialists are trying to reconstitute these old ideas; what matters is deprivation as such', so you get people in Help the Aged, the Child Poverty Action Group, internationally inspired forms of charity, and so on.*

Now it seems to me that the question we have to face is: which of these four characteristics, and in what kind of relationship to one another, matter to us as socialists? We didn't have to ask that question in the past, because we believed that they went together, but now that we know they don't, we have to. And when we keep on being told by certain people that the nature of class hasn't changed, it just prevents us from having to face this profoundly difficult, disturbing, but necessary question.

Question 6: *I feel bad about introducing nasty thoughts into this cosy atmosphere, but what I feel has been done here – and it is hardly what we need – is a softening up, or transformation, of our positive ideals as socialists: namely, that there's an urgency to overcome the capitalist economic system in which we currently live. And I must say I find it quite disturbing that in the face of millions of people starving, in the face of the West gearing up for nuclear war and in the face of ecological catastrophes, if Raphael Samuel takes great delight in reversing the 11th thesis of Marx, I find that that is possibly an Oxford attitude. I just want to know: do the people on the panel feel that there is still an urgency, a need to overcome capitalism even though we all agree that there is no guarantee that it will be possible?*

Stuart Hall: What would the answer 'yes' do for you? It is an invitation to make a ritual incantation. It is like going to the socialist doctor and asking him to tell you something to make you sleep better at night. Of course it's urgent. Of course it's the most important historical question. But you have to get past that desire merely to reaffirm, to the harsher questions: Will it happen? How can it happen? In the real world, as we know it? Does it look as if it's going to happen now more than it did a hundred years ago? And if it doesn't, why not? Those are the difficult questions. Lodged in there is, of course, the thing that makes us not belong to the New Right: the notion that it has to be changed. But the real questions, the hard questions, don't begin there, I'm sorry. I don't think they begin with a testimony of how important it is. The real questions begin with how? Who? When? With what? Under what agenda? What difference would that make? That is where the politics begins.

Sixth Questioner: *The question of whether there's a threat to humanity as such might provide an answer to the question 'What will substitute for class as an agency for socialist policy?', for example.*

Stuart Hall: I think now you are offering another question. You are not now asking a question about what is the urgency, you are actually proposing a debate about the different kinds of socialist agencies – that humanity in general, not class, will make that transformation. We could debate that with profit for a very long time, but it's a different question, and I am not sure that it has been absent from what people have been saying. People have been talking about either the transformations associated with the older definitions of class which sustained a certain form and language of socialist politics, or about the diversity of social and class identities and the diversity of arenas in which a socialist politics for the twenty-first century will have to be constructed. So although we may not have had a very detailed discussion about where that intersects with the concerns that you've identified, we have actually been thinking about what the form of such a politics might be which could match your sense of urgency. I don't want to sound 'cosy' about it, but I don't think we've been as far away from the real political problems underlying your question as you suggested.

Charles Taylor: I would like to say more about this question. You mentioned three things: ecological crisis, nuclear war, and Third World poverty. Is capitalism responsible for all those? What's ruining Lake Baikal now – capitalism? Who is the arms race between – capitalist powers only? The Third World case is stronger, but it is not the only thing that's producing Third World poverty. We could get rid of capitalism, have a Soviet system, and we'd ruin the Great Lakes faster than we're doing it now – because that's what they're doing to Lake Baikal. I think your question is predicated on a false belief; I also think that vast numbers of the electorate in our societies believe correctly that it's a false belief. It's an obstacle to overcoming capitalism to propound socialism on the basis of that belief, because you just lose credibility with this argument. So I would turn it round. This kind of position is actually retarding the overcoming of capitalism – if we can look forward to that. I'd really turn it round.

Raphael Samuel: I'd like to take issue with what Gerry Cohen said [Question 5]. When I read the documents from the Russian Revolution of 1917, I am always amazed by the astonishing way in which soldiers and people in Petrograd described themselves as proletarian. In this deeply unproletarianized country, where the working class actually managed to disappear three years later, the language of being working-class spread like wildfire at the moment of revolution, both in the February Revolution and the October Revolution. The idea that the proletariat was the immense majority of the population was probably never true in any country. Class analysis is always constituted in relations of opposition. It doesn't correspond to some sociological or, for that matter, economically measurable facts.

There was no rational moment of Marxism from which we've now departed; it always involved the imposition of a unified imaginative concept of what society was. Of course what Stuart says is right, but unfortunately the points of actual argument are tied more and more to something that is actually anachronistic, but that's not because a language of majority or even a language of class is less appropriate now than it was in the past. In fact, it is probably more appropriate now than when world revolution was actually on the agenda in 1917.

Question 7: *I'd like to bring up two things. The first is about the session in which I participated this morning and which was probably the most eventful and explosive of the conference. One sister got very angry at the way women still seem to get silenced, not only thirty years ago in the New Left, but even now.*

Now although there has been much talk of difference, and of the need to take different experiences seriously – the experiences of Blacks, of women, of gays, and so on – it seems to me that this always remains a sort of gesturing towards these different experiences, but the recognition of difference does not go beyond that. It's a recognition that to me seems very nominal and does not imply real changes. We need two kinds of change: practical and theoretical.

First, as a practical matter, structures of discussion have to change so as to make it easier for women to participate.

Second, the conceptual framework within which we think has to be changed. In trying to rethink socialism, it has to be recognized that if we talk about things like exploitation, there's no unified phenomenon of exploitation. There are very different forms of exploitation with regard to different groups. One form applies to women, one applies to Blacks, one applies to the handicapped, one applies to the Third World as opposed to the First. So 'Socialist Man' is out, but what's also out is a whole way of relying on a unified conceptual apparatus.

It's very difficult to rethink issues, but I think this is really where we have to start now if we don't want to stay at the level of some kind of gesturing towards later social movements, the advances which they have brought us, and the points which they have made. I don't think we have made any progress unless we actually realize how central these changes are. So maybe what we should take home from this conference is the wish to go into these issues much more, and to do what the New Left was trying to do: to rethink issues and to readdress foundations. But we'll have to do it in different ways, since history has proceeded for thirty years, and we should have learned from some of the mistakes and some of the silences of the New Left.

Stuart Hall: I agree very much with what you say, but I don't know why you haven't heard it in what people have been saying. You say that feminism has made no conceptual or theoretical difference to how people talk, but the entire debate in this session, which is about difference, about the fragmentation of political and social identities, is the consequence of the break which feminism has made in my whole way of conceptualizing politics. The fact that one doesn't name that doesn't mean nothing has changed. So I think it's a question of whether you haven't actually been hearing the impact of the changes you are pointing to, simply because they haven't been literally identified in the form you've been led by your formation and generation to expect. These deep misunderstandings across political generations have been going on all day.

But the second point is this: I had a problem about the session this morning, and I'll state it honestly. I thought the issue that was raised about the absence of feminism, about an inattention to gender – and indeed about a complete silence around questions of sexuality in the politics of the early New Left – is a very profound question, and it was right (and will be productive) for it to be explosive. It had to be the centre of discussion. But I am afraid I think we discussed it in that session in a deeply unsatisfactory way from which nobody could learn. My own experience is that we moralized the issue so that everybody felt guilty, and nobody actually learned anything.

I don't think the people who were involved in a movement that was blank about feminism in that moment learned from that discussion to begin to understand how that came to be so. And I don't think that younger people, younger feminists, learned from that discussion what it was like to live in a left politics before feminism. Even less did they understand how and why the majority of women of the time in the New Left colluded with, and are often themselves deeply unconscious about, the New Left's sexism. We went today for the easy option – making each other feel guilty, in a riot of moralizing – but avoided the hard option. In addition to learning what you are saying, which is to change the forms in which we talk to one another, we also have some other problems – about how to engage in that discussion, not in a way that evades it but in a way from which we could all actually learn something.

I could have said the same thing about race. In a very real way, the early New Left was often quite blank about black politics in Britain, though it became much more sensitive. I would love, at some point, to look at the ways in which that awareness came into our agenda and the ways in which it didn't. But I don't think there is much point in raising that in such a way as to make people who were involved in the New Left simply feel: 'My God, I didn't think about racism, *mea culpa!* – sackcloth and ashes, bread and water.' That just demobilizes people. You can't do anything about the past except think about what an awful experience it was, and how could you ever have done that to anybody else. So I do think we still have a great deal to learn, collectively, about how we can engage in such a discussion without taking people off the hook, but so that we can collectively learn from it in order to transform our political practice.

Raphael Samuel: I would like to say something on that. The journal on which I work, the *History Workshop* journal, calls itself a journal of socialist and feminist historians, and the particular struggle that took place was formed out of a similarly explosive session at a History Workshop in 1970. And we still live with that in our collective, even though we've made it a matter of principle that we have equal representation of men and women. So I think that what Jean McCrindle said in the earlier session about the ways in which women were silenced – which was said, after all, from her own experience as an active organizer of the Scottish New Left clubs – was extremely valuable. And in practice – think of the parliamentary front bench which, in an election year, had not a single woman on it; think of organization after organization in the labour movement (less so now in the trade unions) – again and again, things are set up in such a way that you have, as we have now, an all-male platform. Now we have to work very hard to prevent that happening, we have to work against the grain of that happening, and I do think that's an elementary duty in any socialist organization. And the symbolic here actually matters a great deal. It is not right that people should face all-male platforms in organizations that claim to be representing men and women.

I have had one or two uncomfortable moments in what I think has been a very heartening discussion. There was one particular speaker who talked about, first of all, the threat to the world ecology, and then said: 'Well, if it isn't ecology, can there be something else?' My sense (which may be a misreading of what he was saying) is that he was more concerned with what could be a totalizing politics than with an urgent sense of issues. There is a mode which I recognize as being something peculiar to men, which is a way of constructing politics that really is very remote from the subjective experience. I think that the early New Left, and *ULR* in particular, was rather sympathetic to what became later feminism. But it is not just a matter of formal recognition, nor even of changing concepts, but actually of a tone, an urgency and a form of address. For example, I know that my wife's way of addressing a political battle is qualitatively different from mine – and so it should be. A socialist movement ought to have equal space for both those voices.

Question 8 [Malcolm McEwen]: *I thought perhaps it was about time somebody who was on* The New Reasoner *had a word, as we haven't had much of a look-in for the last little while. What I want to say has really got nothing to do with* The New Reasoner, *except that it's back to the old question of what we didn't think about. Charles Taylor has just said that if we had a socialist system, we'd get Lake Baikals everywhere because that is how socialism behaves: just as capitalism behaves. He's quite right. In socialist theory, and in Soviet theory and practice, there has so far been no room for the concept that part of socialism is in fact looking after not only the people, but the environment in which we live – which is in fact the basis for life, and without which none of us can have a living or a life at all. What this points to is the need to revise socialist theory, because in my way of thinking capitalist theory and practice make it much more difficult to look after the environment because capitalism operates for profit; it operates to exploit the environment as well as human beings. That's an element which was also, in a way, missing in Marx. From my reading of Marx and Engels, I get the impression that Engels would in fact have been in the very forefront of the ecological movement, had he been alive in the 1960s.*

Question 9: *The title of this conference is 'Out of Apathy', so not knowing very much about the group that organized it, I came thinking that it was going to be a sort of reproach to my generation for the lack of activism on student campuses and for our general materialist self-interest. But instead of a call to organize, what I've been hearing is a call to analyse: let's just all get together and think. But I would like to know what the issues are about which we should organize, and I'd like to ask each member of the panel to list what they think are the most critical political challenges facing the left, and in brief what they think should be done about them.*

Question 10: *The paradigm of the socialist that everyone is talking about is still that of an actor, an agent. I wonder if there could be an understanding of a socialist where we could also allow for a socialist to be a spectator, not really an actor. Perhaps at a given time, in a given place, in a certain context, we may not be able to have any answer or any solution to the problem with which we are faced. Perhaps then we should take a back seat and not do anything about it, or not think that we must have a solution to it. What I have in mind is the problem that we are facing of diverse cultures, and in particular of conflict between two dif-ferent cultures, as in India, where I come from. I think that any position the left takes there leads to disaster. Maybe we should have some view of a socialist in which it is not necessary that a socialist is always doing* *something, or taking a position – where you are almost a non-participant.*

Question 11: *Does the panel really feel that it's done justice to the movement it's representing? There is an important economic dimension to the work of the New Left, although it is a weakness that it hasn't been thought through as part of the whole cultural rethinking of socialism. But in a sense, the panel isn't representing that dimension of the argument. And in my own daily work, that dimension of the argument is one of the most crucial.*

Secondly, I wonder whether the panel has done justice to itself. Couldn't speakers have said more about their own experiences of struggle? I don't want to make an anti-intellectual argument, but haven't they abstracted to such an extent that it's no longer possible to talk about positive concrete struggles of the kind many of us are engaged in?

Raphael Samuel: (response to Question 9): The thing that's exciting to me about the meeting today is that it was organized by people from many different countries – very much how our New Left began. And that means that subversive or revolutionary ideas will circulate far afield. We can't foresee the different ways in which things that people have picked up today, or in your Socialist Discussion Group, will be taken, domesticated and transformed when they are taken across the sea. So I think that's one very excellent thing about the day. It also means that any kind of agenda – in answer to the question 'What do you think is the most urgent, or a priority now?' – must be very partial. I have a number of issues, which just come from local experience. My first would be the defence of the inner city against a kind of regeneration going on from an unholy alliance of office developers, conservationists, Mrs Thatcher's government and, in the part of London in which I live, European, Japanese and American capital about to take over the Isle of Dogs. That would involve, for me, socialists taking a much more active role in local politics, which was absolutely paralysed for ten years by a dog-fight between right and left which has delivered my local council to a white, racist, Liberal council. It would mean having a more generous range of sympathies than socialists have had in the past. It would mean, for example, defending small businesses – the Bengali businesses which happen to be the heart of our particular district, a kind of late version of a very ancient but very thriving and flourishing textile industry. That's one of the things I'd like to campaign about.

Another would be the defence of education – partly the defence of liberal values in education – at a point at which the very idea of education as a social good in itself is being attacked by the Education Secre-

tary's bill and by all the multiple pressures which teachers, lecturers and
every sector in education has had to suffer. One of the uncomfortable
but valuable questions today has been 'have you helped Thatcherism?'
Now one area in which, for the most honourable reasons, we've actually
helped to prepare the ground for an attack on education has been in the
post-1968 questioning of the pieties of liberal education – demands for a
more relevant education.

Now we find ourselves hoist with our own petard. Somebody from
the Department of Education says: 'Well, some people are fitted to be
artists, and others to be ballet dancers, and others to be plumbers, and
others to go into subaltern positions in the new financial-services
industry', and by some financial wizardry, with decreasing funds, all
these needs are going to be met without wasting a single penny. The
result is that the whole of English education has been made a misery and
the sense of worth, certainly among teachers, has been thoroughly
undermined. In fact, the whole idea of public service has been undermined, which means that anybody who works in the public sector, in the
still watches of the night, has doubts about whether they're needed. I
think there's a programme for education which involves defending both
the gains that socialists and libertarians have made in education in the
last twenty or thirty years, but also of an older inheritance. Those are two
of my priorities.

(Response to Question 8): About the politics of the environment:
different people will want to agitate this in different ways. It seems to me
absolutely consonant with a Labour Party which, after all, legislated the
Green Belt and which spent its early years bicycling people out of the
cities to enjoy the countryside, to take those issues up. Of course, Chuck
Taylor is absolutely right that the Soviet Union is even more ruthless in
its exploitation of natural resources, and certainly more ruthless in its
treatment of indigenous populations than capitalism is, but we happen
to be in the capitalist sector of the world, so it's our job to take up those
issues in a socialist way. But I wouldn't worry too much about labels.
One of the good things that the New Left did was not to worry too much
about whether or not you could put the socialist hat on something.
Campaign for something, and if that wins recruits for socialism, fine. If it
doesn't, that's still fine – the campaign needs waging.

Stuart Hall (response to Question 10): Yes, there is always a moment
in the politics of the left when doing nothing is probably the best thing.
There are always issues where what position to take is not at all obvious
or clear-cut, where each alternative has so many costs that you can't see
what advantages would be gained by giving all your energies to sustaining

the position. I think that is just in the nature of political struggle in all its messy contingency. But I suppose underneath your questions is something which I can't give up, and that is, I think, to do with the notion of passivity. I think that not only tolerating passivity, but seeing other people as passive recipients of processes, is one of the cultural processes that consolidates conservatism with a small c.

I don't want to endorse the picture of the continually engaged militant activist, because I don't think that is a very appropriate image either. Most people I know who have lived politics like that live it for about three and a half years, then they give it up, exhausted and disillusioned, for the rest of their lives. Nevertheless, we must retain the notion that people can do more than society ever asks of them; they have capacities they have not yet imagined or touched. That will make them active social beings, although being a socialist is not always summed up in terms of activism. In that wider sense, democracy, not just socialism, is an intrinsic part of my conception of politics.

(Response to Question 9): About the question of where we should mobilize: I am sure you will be frustrated because I won't answer your question. I could give you a whole range of arenas around which I think one ought now to organize and mobilize, but still there would always be in my mind the larger question of how those particular struggles connect with a larger socialist project. So in a sense I am not dodging the question but this other question, the question of hegemonic strategy, is the question I want to hold in front of your mind just now.

Let me take an area in which I have been involved for twenty years: the arena of black politics. Now, you know, one could at the drop of the hat name you ten fronts which are simply going to have to be defended in the next five years against the rolling tide of popular racism. Still, one must continue to ask what the articulations are between black politics and class politics in this society. I don't want to collude in presenting organizing, activism and mobilization as a substitute for worrying about those other, deeper questions of strategy and political conception.

Now, of course, some of those questions may never be solved. And in the meantime, until they're solved, we're going to have to turn up wearing fifty different hats, and stick our fingers in fifty different dykes in the next month, defend fifty different 'good causes'. That's life. But behind that is the question: is this preventing them from absolutely rolling over you for ever? Or is this beginning to shift the relations of forces, so that we begin moving on to our own agenda, not their agenda; not just defending something so that we don't slip back into barbarism, but actually getting together the resources by which we might project a more just and humane future? That's the underlying question that I thought it was

right to centre on today – not to suggest that other questions are unimportant, just that they are not what could be most usefully pinpointed
today.

(Response to Question 11): That brings me to the last question, which
is whether we have done ourselves justice. Well, I'm sure we haven't
done ourselves justice. We have probably been too modest, too self-
critical. There are vast numbers of areas which we touched, and which
we haven't projected to you. It's true, of course, that all of us could have
spent all the time talking about political struggles and political arenas in
which we have been deeply engaged. I am sorry my friend from the New
Right has departed – I now spend my entire political life thinking about
what is different about Thatcherism.
    The notion that there is no writing on the left about how different
Thatcherism is, as a formation on the right, from old-style conservatism
is really news to me, because I seem to have been writing about nothing
else since 1975 – about how different it is, and why it is different, and
why the left has to understand its specificity, how it articulates old
elements with new elements, how it intrudes into the ground of the
politics of the left, how it has occupied our space. And if that is not
entirely new, it is certainly pretty important. So of course we could have
talked against that background, but it would have been a totally different
occasion.
    I thought what today, in a sense, gave us the luxury of being able to
do, was to say to you: 'You know us in many of those other mani-
festations, but here is something you don't know – we have been thinking about some of these ideas since about 1955.' It's allowed us to
remind you that socialist politics isn't born again every day; it takes
place within a set of traditions, within a formation.
    Actually, I really quite agree with a lot of things I wrote a very long
time ago. You know, the first political article I ever wrote was about
'The New Conservatism' [ULR 1] – would you believe that? It was
about the other new Conservatives – Butler and the lot; and how
Thorneycroft and the rest had transformed the Conservative Party. And,
bloody hell, it is 1987 and I'm saying exactly the same thing: a new lot
are in and they're transforming conservatism again, and there's a new,
new, new conservatism. I brought a ton of bricks tumbling down on my
head when I wrote a piece called 'A Sense of Classlessness' [ULR 5],
but actually I still think there's a sense of classlessness about. I actually
think 'a sense of classlessness' is part of what keeps Thatcherism going. I
think the 'transformation of class society' is a big game now. So I have to
confess to you that political formations do matter, and it is useful to
spend a few moments thinking about them.

However, I urge you also not to be too mesmerized by and stuck in 'history'. I do invite you to understand the role of historical memory in politics. We came from somewhere. We are both confined by, but were also produced by, a particular historical conjuncture. That moment will never come again. Anybody who turned up today to hear that it is going to repeat itself, either as tragedy or as farce, will be severely disappointed. No, I'm four-square with Heraclitus: you can't step in the same river twice. But that doesn't matter. What matters is some sense of *continuity through transformation* – of political allegiances which won't go away, of bedrock reference points – which does allow us to say something about the present conjuncture.

Charles Taylor (response to Question 10): I'd just like to make a small point. I understood this question about doing nothing slightly differently. I understood it as: Are there not certain situations where there just is no solution – like certain Communist struggles, where you can't think of anything you can do that won't make the situation worse? There are such situations. This is where what Raph was saying earlier comes in. We have to reverse Marx's 11th thesis there, and not have the attitude that we are regressing when we turn back to try to understand the world. It is probable that we just don't understand the roots of that kind of thing at all well, and that what we've had in the way of general theories in the socialist movement have been lamentably inadequate to understand that, and the same goes for racism and other such phenomena. At that point, to sit back and understand it, and really make progress in understanding it, would be perhaps the most useful thing to do. There I entirely agree. And that is really what I would say to the other questioner up there – part of the reason why we have not been very concrete here is that we come from different countries. I could bore you for hours about Canadian politics, but we wanted to talk at a different level here.

I have felt again and again, in the particular political movements and political struggles I have been in, that there were very deep blockages to our doing anything good and useful sometimes, and even cases where we did things that were catastrophic – that had to do with our not understanding, or not having sufficiently liberated ourselves from, deep crippling beliefs. Standing back and thinking about them philosophically was something we did far too little of. There may be a great deal of political goofing off and not turning up to the meeting, and so on, but it hasn't been in the name of philosophical reflection. We really need more of that. I frankly immensely appreciated this invitation and enjoyed the possibility today of being able to go into some of those issues, because I think we just don't do that enough.

Index of Contributors

LINDSAY ANDERSON wrote for *Universities and Left Review* (*ULR*). His Free Cinema films include *If*, *O Lucky Man*, and *Britannia Hospital*.

MICHAEL BARRATT BROWN wrote for *The New Reasoner* (*NR*). He was until recently Principal of Northern College.

SHEILA BENSON was secretary of the London New Left Club. She now teaches sociology at Lancashire Polytechnic.

LAWRENCE DALY was founder of the Fife Socialist League. He retired as General Secretary of the National Union of Mineworkers in 1984.

TREVOR GRIFFITHS wrote for *ULR*. His plays include *The Party*, *Comedians*, and *Occupations*.

STUART HALL was a co-editor of *ULR* and the first editor of *New Left Review* (*NLR*). He is now Professor of Sociology at the Open University.

JOHN HUGHES co-authored the New Left pamphlet *A Socialist Wages Plan* and was a frequent contributor to *NR*. He is now Principal of Ruskin College.

MERVYN JONES wrote for *NR*. His novels include *Holding On* and he has recently published his memoirs, *Chances*.

MALCOLM McEWEN was a contributor to *NR* and on the editorial board of *NLR*. He is now active in the conservation of the National Parks.

MICHAEL RUSTIN was on the editorial board of *NLR*. He teaches sociology at North East London Polytechnic.

RAPHAEL SAMUEL was co-editor of *ULR*. He now teaches history at Ruskin College.

LYNNE SEGAL teaches psychology at Middlesex Polytechnic. Her writings include *Is the Future Female?*

CLANCY SIGAL was on the editorial board of *ULR*. He now teaches English at the University of California at Los Angeles.

CHARLES TAYLOR was co-editor of *ULR*. He is now a Fellow of All Souls College, Oxford and Professor of Political and Social Theory at McGill University.

DOROTHY WEDDERBURN was a contributor to *NR*. She is now Principal of Royal Holloway and Bedford New College, University of London.

PETER WORSLEY was on the editorial board of *NR*. Until recently he was Professor of Sociology at Manchester University.

The Editors

ROBIN ARCHER, an Australian, was active in the Australian trade-union movement. He is now doing research on economic democracy.

DIEMUT BUBECK, a West German, former member of 'Die Grünen', is working on a materialist conception of justice and feminist issues.

HANJO GLOCK, a West German, was active in the West German peace and Green movements. He is now doing research on the later philosophy of Wittgenstein.

LESLEY JACOBS, a Canadian, was involved in Canadian student campaigns. He does research on rights and distributive justice.

SETH MOGLEN, a US American, was involved in the Nuclear Disarmament movement in the USA, and was until recently engaged in research on British politics.

ADAM STEINHOUSE, a Canadian, was active in the Central America solidarity campaigns. He is researching workers' demands and the state, with specific reference to post-liberation France.

DANIEL WEINSTOCK, a Canadian, was active in the Canadian universities' South Africa divestment campaign. He is now working on the political and moral philosophy of Kant.

Printed by Printforce, United Kingdom